New Directions in Corporate Strategy

GARRY TWITE, Senior Lecturer in Finance at the Australian Graduate School of Management, University of New South Wales, and MICHAEL O'KEEFFE, National Business Manager—Produce, of Franklins Limited, worked with Rabobank Australia Limited to assemble a team of experts on corporate strategy from the Australian Graduate School of Management and provide this crisp, readable summary of the key ideas which are shaping corporate strategy into the next decade.

New Directions in Corporate Strategy

Edited by
Garry Twite and Michael O'Keeffe

ALLEN & UNWIN

First published in 2000 by
Allen & Unwin
9 Atchison Street
St Leonards NSW 1590
Australia
Phone: (61 2) 8425 0100
Fax: (61 2) 9906 2218
E-mail: frontdesk@allen-unwin.com.au
Web: http://www.allen-unwin.com.au

National Library of Australia
Cataloguing-in-Publication entry:

New directions in corporate strategy.

Bibliography.
Includes index.
ISBN 1 86508 207 4.

1. Strategic planning. 2. Business planning. 3. Competition.
4. Organisational change. 5. Organisational effectiveness.
6. Strategic alliances (Business). 7. Business networks.
8. Corporations—Growth. I. Twite, Garry.
II. O'Keeffe, Michael, 1951– .

658.4012

Set in 10/13 pt Casablanca by DOCUPRO, Sydney
Printed by Australian Print Group, Maryborough, Vic.

10 9 8 7 6 5 4 3 2 1

Foreword by Rabobank

Rabobank Australia Limited has two aspirations in sponsoring this book. The first is to continue our bank's commitment to investing in knowledge-driven relationships with institutions of excellence, and the Australian Graduate School of Management certainly provides excellent research and education services to the greater Australian business community.

The second aspiration, close to our hearts and core business as bankers, is to invest in the managerial capabilities and intangible asset base of our clients. We believe that financing sustained superior growth is not just about managing a firm's cash flow and balance sheet. An equally important component of financing and risk management is how a firm develops its intellectual capital base, its ability to innovate, the skills and vision of its people, its understanding of customers and the competitive factors influencing the markets in which it operates.

Rabobank is acutely aware of the forces of globalisation: markets are becoming more competitive, transparent, service-oriented and specialised. While our global expertise is in financing the agribusiness, food and health chains, I would commend this book to executives and managers from any sector who are ideas-rich, time-poor, and searching for a management tool to help them meet the challenges of forming and implementing strategy at a business or firm level. The concepts discussed in this book are applicable to public and private organisations, regardless of firm size. They are particularly relevant to executives seeking to understand the forces influencing the value chains in which they operate.

I commend these authors for their vision and expertise. This book will make a significant contribution to our understanding and practice of leading edge strategic concepts.

Cor Broekhuyse
Chief Executive Officer, Rabobank Australia Ltd

Foreword by the Australian Graduate School of Management

This book brings together, under the Australian Graduate School of Management's banner, strategies across many disciplines. It fulfils one of the AGSM's more important missions, which is to maintain communication links between business and academia.

An integral part of the design of this book is to ensure that the reader gets an understanding of the development of the history of strategic thought as it flows across all disciplines. It also provides a current perspective of each discipline's view of strategy.

A blending of all of these disciplines to give management a set of references they can use in their day-to-day business environment is reinforced by examples taken from the two important value drivers for every firm—knowledge acquisition and corporate reputation.

David Hoare, Chairman,
Australian Graduate School of Management

The AGSM is a School of both The University of Sydney and The University of New South Wales

Contents

Acknowledgments

There are many people who assisted in the preparation of this book. We are indebted to a number of colleagues for their comments on drafts of various papers, particularly to Robin Stonecash for her willingness to provide detailed comments on the completed manuscript and Larissa Taylor for her effort in bringing the project to fruition. We should also mention three individuals who contributed significantly to the genesis of this book: Michael O'Keeffe who conceived the notion of a collection of individual papers that discussed the enduring concepts within the various management disciplines, using strategy as the link; and Fred Hilmer and Robin Edwards who together proposed a book which could present the papers as a single unit. Robin Edwards should also be thanked for her perseverance in coordinating the demands and excuses of fifteen authors. Thanks also go to publishers Allen & Unwin, particularly John Iremonger, for believing in the book.

Figures and tables

FIGURES

TABLES

Contributors

Timothy M. Devinney is Associate Professor at the Australian Graduate School of Management and Director of the Centre for Corporate Change. He has published more than thirty articles in leading journals and four books, including *The Essence of Corporate Strategy: Theory for Modern Decision Making* (Allen & Unwin, 1997) with Professor Jeremy Davis. His two forthcoming books are *Theory and Methodology in Strategy* (Kluwer) and *Managing the Global Corporation* (with J. de la Torré and Y. Doz, McGraw-Hill). He is an editor of the *Australian Journal of Management* and on the editorial board of several leading academic journals.

Grahame Dowling is Professor of Marketing at the Australian Graduate School of Management. His research has been published in the world's leading academic journals and in a book titled *Corporate Reputations: Strategies for Developing the Corporate Brand* (Kogan Page, 1994). In 1997 Grahame was named The Distinguished Marketing Researcher in Australia and New Zealand for his work on the adoption and diffusion of new products and he is a frequent speaker at academic, industry, and in-company conferences both in Australia and overseas on these and other marketing topics.

Frederick Hilmer is Chief Executive Officer at Fairfax Holdings Limited. Until recently he was Dean and Professor of Management at the Australian Graduate School of Management and a Director of Port Jackson Partners Limited. Prior to joining AGSM Fred was a partner of McKinsey & Company for twenty years and for the last nine of those years he managed the Australian practice. In 1991 the Australian Institute of Management awarded him a special John Storey medal for distinguished contribution to the advancement of management thinking in Australia. He has written extensively on strategy, organisation and economic reform and is the author of a number of books, including, *When the Luck Runs Out*, (Harper & Row, 1985) and, *New Games/New Rules* (Angus & Robertson, 1989) and co-authored *Strictly Boardroom* (Information Australia, 1993), *Working Relations* (Business Library, 1993) and *Management Redeemed* (Free Press, 1996).

Robert Marks is an Associate Professor at the Australian Graduate School of Management. Bob has published over 50 papers in such journals as the *Journal of Economic Dynamics & Control*, *Management Science*, *Economics Letters*, and the *Australian Journal of Management*, of which he is currently General Editor.

Ian Marsh is an Associate Professor at the Australian Graduate School of Management. He is the author (with Jean Blondel and Takashi Inoguchi) of *Democracy, Governance and Economic Performance in East and Southeast Asia* (United Nations University Press, forthcoming). Other recent studies include: *Beyond the Two Party System* (Cambridge University Press, 1995) and *Australian Business in the Asia-Pacific Region* (Longmans, 1992).

Pamela D. Morrison is a Senior Lecturer in Marketing at the University of Sydney, and has fifteen years' marketing management experience across a wide spectrum, ranging from NSW Forecasting Manager for Telecom, to Manager of the Centre for Applied Marketing, AGSM. She has published in international journals and her

PhD proposal won the international Institute for the Study of Business Markets Doctoral Support award.

Charlie J. Nelson is Executive Director Advanced Analytical Research at A C Nielsen Australia. His forecasting career started at Telecom Australia (now Telstra) and continued as a consultant for organisations spanning a wide range of industries including retail, financial services, telecommunications and transport. He has enjoyed considerable success in accurately forecasting retail spending and new motor vehicle sales in Australia in difficult economic circumstances.

Michael O'Keeffe is National Business Manager—Produce with Franklins Limited. Prior to joining Franklins in early 1999 Michael was Chief Manager, Agribusiness Advisory and Research Services with Rabo Australia Ltd. Michael is vice-president of the Australian Agribusiness Association and is on the Board of the International Agribusiness Management Association. He is also Adjunct Professor of Value Chain Management at the University of Queensland and is on the Meat, Dairy, Aquaculture Sector Advisory Committee for the CSIRO.

John H. Roberts is the National Australian Bank Professor of Marketing at the Australian Graduate School of Management. His PhD from MIT on new product development won the American Marketing Association's John Howard Award for the top doctorate in the US. Professor Roberts consults extensively and sits on a number of boards. He has won the Distinguished Teaching Award at the AGSM and teaches regularly at Stanford University's Graduate School of Business. He is a Fellow of the Australian Institute of Management, the Australian Marketing Institute and the Australian Institute of Advertising, as well as the US Commonwealth Fund and the UK Twenty First Century Trust.

Peter W. Roberts is an Assistant Professor of Strategy at the Graduate School of Industrial Administration at Carnegie Mellon University. After receiving his PhD in Organizational Analysis from the University of Alberta (Canada), Peter spent three years on the faculty at the AGSM. His research examines the factors that affect firm-level sustained superior financial performance, innovation and sustainable competitive advantage.

Christopher Sauer is Senior Research Fellow in the Fujitsu Centre for Managing Information Technology in Organisations at the Australian Graduate School of Management. His most recent book, co-authored with Philip Yetton, is *Steps to the Future: Fresh Thinking in the Management of IT-Based Organizational Transformation* (Jossey-Bass, 1997). He holds a number of positions in the international community including Deputy-Chair of the International Federation for Information Processing Working Group on the Transfer and Diffusion of IT, and Asia-Pacific Editor for the *Journal of Strategic Information Systems.* In 1998 he led the team that produced the report *Information Technology in the Building and Construction Industry: Current Status and Future Directions* for the Department of Industry, Science and Tourism in Canberra.

Tom Smith is the FAI Professor of Finance and Head of the Accounting and Finance cluster at the Australian Graduate School of Management. He graduated from the University of Queensland with a Masters of Financial Management and received his PhD in Finance from Stanford University in 1990. Tom has lectured and consulted extensively in Australia and the US over the past twenty years and his articles have appeared in leading Australian and overseas journals.

Dennis Turner is Professor of General Management at the Australian Graduate School of Management. He has recently finished a research program in the AGSM's Centre for Corporate Change on the impact of personal and corporate competencies on change effectiveness. He has published in this field and contributed to conferences organised by the Strategic Management Society, the US Academy of Management and the Harvard Business School. A book he co-authored with Dr Michael Crawford, *Change Power: Capabilities that Drive Corporate Renewal*, was published in 1998 (Business & Professional Publishing).

Garry Twite is a Senior Lecturer in Finance at the Australian Graduate School of Management and has been a visiting assistant professor at the Anderson Graduate School of Management at the

University of California, Los Angeles and Hong Kong University of Science and Technology. He is the Deputy General Editor of the *Australian Journal of Management* and is an ad hoc referee for this and several other journals. Garry has published in leading Australian journals and is one of the authors of the successful text *Corporate Finance* (Holt, Rinehart and Winston, 1993), which is used throughout Australia. He has been a consultant to numerous companies, banks and accounting firms and is a member of several professional associations, including the Accounting Association of Australia and New Zealand, American Finance Association and Asia Pacific Finance Association.

David Wilson has been the Alvin H. Clemens Professor of Entrepreneurial Studies at the Pennsylvania State University since 1993. From 1975 until 1993 he was Professor of Marketing and from 1982 until present he has been the Managing Director of the Institute for the Study of Business Markets, one of the leading international academic research centres for business-to-business marketing. Professor Wilson was the founding editor of the *Journal of Business-to-Business Marketing* and served as editor until 1995 when he moved to Associate Editor. He has served on numerous editorial boards and was Section Editor of the *Journal of Marketing* from 1981 to 1984. Professor Wilson is an author or co-author of over 200 books, articles and papers in business marketing.

1

Introduction

GARRY TWITE AND MICHAEL O'KEEFFE

Strategy is at the dawn of a new era. There has been a fundamental shift in business strategy thinking over the last decade, however, this change has been difficult to discern for two reasons. The first reason is the plethora of management 'styles' which has created a high level of background 'noise'. The second reason is that while strategic thinking has changed, the objectives, basic approach and outcomes of the strategy process have remained constant over this period. The objective of the strategy is still to gain a competitive advantage and achieve superior performance on a sustainable basis. Achieving the right fit between the organisation and the external environment remains the secret to success, and the outcome of choosing products and services to compete in particular markets is also unchanged.

Despite these constants, our understanding of why some firms are more competitive than others, and consequently insights into the role and task of managers, has undergone a profound change. The objective of this book is to cut through the peripheral noise and to present the enduring changes in management thinking across a range of disciplines relevant to management practitioners.

In essence, the focus has shifted from the industry, to the recognition that the keys to success largely lie within the firm and its relationship with its stakeholders. This seemingly trivial statement has profound implications to managers—from corporate strategy to operational details. For example, this book provides managers with a robust foundation for tackling challenges as diverse as:

- crafting strategies within competition policy guidelines;
- developing the knowledge base;
- developing the corporate brand;
- developing and implementing IT management;
- effective leadership of corporate change;
- integrating finance and strategy.

THE 1980s VIEW OF STRATEGY

A decade ago there was a high degree of consensus and confidence in the view that industry attractiveness provided the answers to the key strategy question of 'Why do some firms consistently outperform their competitors?'.

Under this paradigm, the main task of managers was to choose which industry to compete in, as industry was the main determinant of profitability. The logical progression is the view of the manager buying and selling businesses to build a portfolio of businesses in attractive industries. Escaping portfolios during the late 1980s was extremely difficult. Resources were tradeable: bought and sold.

As industry was the key driver of performance it also followed that it was critical for firms to respond quickly to changes in the external environment.

Not surprisingly, talk of a strategy-implementation gap started to surface and practitioners, both management and consultants, shifted their attention to implementation and efficiency challenges.

It therefore comes as no surprise to recall the number of adaptation-driven management responses such as quicker response time, and implementation fads such as total quality management (TQM), re-engineering, downsizing, and catching up with leading edge competitors through benchmarking-type initiatives. This focus on 'How can we do what we currently do better?' meant that the more important strategy question 'What should we be doing?' was neglected.

Strategy and competition policy

The 'industry' view, which is based on industrial organisation economics, had a number of profound implications from a public policy perspective.

Industrial organisation is the study of the nature and outcomes of competition, with the underlying assumption that superior profitability comes from impeding competitive forces. From a public policy perspective, if superior firm performance comes from circumventing competition, then the role of public policy must be to sponsor competition.

For the policy maker, the most significant factors in determining the nature of competition policy are the role of government in influencing competition, the nature of the process to be used by government, its relationship with business and the approach adopted to resolve conflicts between competitive outcomes and social goals.

The irony is that business took to Porter[1] like a duck to water without fully understanding the public policy implications. It is difficult for business to present its case to competition policy regulators using a framework that is based on a theory that assumes superior performance must be based on anti-competitive behaviour.

The response of governments is to introduce a policy regime that sponsors competition—at a naive level—the assumption being that 'more competition is better'. Hence, the focus in many countries on competition policy.

To understand the impact of competition policy on business requires an examination of the role of economic efficiency and its relationship to consumer welfare.

The chapters by Hilmer and Marsh take up these issues. Hilmer introduces us to this theme, focusing on identifying the components of competition policy. He identifies six components, ranging from limiting anti-competitive behaviour, through reforming the structure of public monopolies to fostering competitive neutrality between government and business. Using this framework Hilmer explores three issues in Chapter 2:

1 the nature and extent of competition required to achieve the objectives of competition policy—termed 'effective competition';
2 the effect and appropriateness of different regulatory models; and
3 the impact of competition on social goals.

His general conclusion is one of conflict within the literature. We still have a lot to learn about the nature of competition and the impact of regulation. To use Hilmer's words, is competition 'a fragile flower or a tough weed'?

In Chapter 3 Marsh follows on this line of discussion, focusing on the nature of the business–government relationship. He considers the simple question, in setting competition policy, 'Should we adopt a competitive or collaborative model of the business–government relationship?' Marsh concludes that, if Australia's future lies in innovation and growth, this is best achieved under a collaborative model.

A reconciliation of the views of Hilmer and Marsh lies in the definition of the objectives of competition policy. Marsh sees these objectives as including the sponsoring of growth and innovation.

While relevant to the policy debate, the question of which model to adopt in setting competition policy and in turn the way firms modify behaviour under alternative regulatory regimes are not central to management. The central issue for management remains—is it industry competitive structure that determines profitability?

During the late 1980s a number of academics began to question the prevailing view and new theories offering fresh insights for practising managers were developed. The pendulum began to swing back towards the notion that factors internal to the firm had a more important influence on profitability than industry structure.

For example, a recent empirical study has shown that firm level effects are five times as important as industry on profitability.[2] In general, 'firm' accounts for 45–55 per cent of variance and 'industry' 8–10 per cent. Another study co-authored by the high priest of the

1980s view, Harvard's Michael Porter, has also confirmed the importance of firm: in this study McGahan and Porter find that industry and business unit effects account for 19 per cent and 32 per cent, respectively, of the aggregate variance in profitability.[3]

Needless to say, the debate on the relative importance of firm and industry continues within academia. But the important point for industry is that there is a dynamic relationship between organisational capabilities and industry level competition. The market environment shapes strategies and capabilities, and the performance of firms with different capabilities and strategies in turn influences the competitive environment.

THE 1990s VIEW OF STRATEGY

Resource-based view

The body of literature focusing on the firm is known as the resource-based theory of the firm, and was brought to the attention of managers in a 1984 *Strategic Management Journal* article 'A Resource-based View of the Firm' by Wernerfelt.[4]

This switch in focus to the firm had strategy researchers asking the more fundamental questions:

- Why do firms exist in the form they do?
- Why do we find different types of organisations competing in the same market?
- Why do firms consistently differ in terms of performance?

These questions had as their genesis the study of the nature of the firm, where economists sought to answer what seem to be relatively simple, but fundamental questions.

Chapter 4 by Marks lets us examine the role economics played in increasing our understanding of the nature of the firm. Marks introduces us to the concept of assets being specific to the firm, a concept which is the foundation of the resource-based theory of the firm.

Chapter 5 by Devinney, details how the resource-based theory of the firm evolved and its implications for corporate strategy.

Figure 1.1 Description of core capabilities

Core capabilities:

- are valuable across a range of products and markets;
- are deeply embedded in the organisation;
- are socially complex;
- are widely dispersed throughout the organisation;
- probably exist in clusters of competencies;
- need to be supported by value systems that encourage change;
- must be evaluated relative to competitors;
- are in the context of a target market segment.

Namely, that sustainable advantage requires that firms possess resources that are:

- unique;
- lack a substitute;
- flexible or dynamic; and
- durable.

The implication is that under the resource-based theory of the firm, sustainable competitive advantage is based on resources and assets—core capabilities—that are not easily bought, substituted or copied (see Figure 1.1). In fact, the firm can be defined as a collection of dynamically evolving capabilities and these capabilities establish the boundaries and growth of the firm. Success derives from the match between capabilities and the target market. Long-term success is based on resources and capabilities that competitors cannot copy.

The essence of this line of thinking is to develop resources or capabilities that are not easily traded, or copied or substituted by competitors. By definition, these capabilities will often be the intangible assets of the firm, will be deeply embedded in the organisation and will be socially complex. The key role for managers is to create and nurture these capabilities. *Resources are built, not bought.*

The chapters by Devinney and Dowling discuss two examples of assets that are both developed over time and potential sources of sustainable advantage, namely organisational knowledge and corporate reputation.

In Chapter 5, Devinney suggests that of all the intangible resources that may be held by the firm, organisational knowledge is the most valuable, but also the most difficult to articulate, understand, develop and transfer. He concludes that for a firm to maintain a sustainable advantage through organisational knowledge it must exhibit the three 'c's':

1 *creativity* in its ability to solve problems;
2 *comprehensiveness* in its ability to gather, retain and synthesise information; and
3 *consensus* in its decision-making know-how.

Dowling identifies corporate reputation as another important source of sustainable advantage in Chapter 6. He commences his discussion with a warning, namely, it is most important to remember that reputation is not a single issue, the various groups of stakeholders in the firm (security holders, employees, customers, suppliers and government) are likely to have different images and hence, reputations of the firm. Forgetting this is a mistake often made by management.

In discussing the creation and maintenance of a reputation, Dowling identifies four essential building blocks:

1 identify what your organisation stands for;
2 identify the factors that determine your reputation;
3 don't do anything likely to destroy your reputation; and finally, and possibly most important,
4 communicate to both internal and external stakeholders.

An implication of the chapters by both Devinney and Dowling is that sustainable advantage must be developed through time—it is dynamic. It is this dynamic aspect of sustainable advantage that Roberts takes up in Chapter 7 on the influence of Schumpeter on corporate strategy.

Peter Roberts highlights the point that sustainable advantage is a dynamic and fragile concept. At the centre of the resource-based theory of the firm is the role of entrepreneurial vision in creating sustainable advantage and the threat of competitor imitation in destroying that advantage. Roberts argues that these insights owe a large debt to the writings of Schumpeter, namely his argument that the concepts of innovative and imitative dynamics are more important components of competition than simply price competition.

The recognition of competitor imitation and its relationship to sustainable advantage question how the firm defends its 'advantage'. Chapter 8 by John Roberts, Nelson and Morrison explores this question, using the example of a telephone company's defence against a new entrant.

The dynamic aspects of the creation and defence of sustainable advantage are suggestive of a process of corporate change. As the firm goes about building sustainable advantage, so to do we often observe the firm itself changing. If this is the case then the value created by building sustainable advantage can be destroyed by ineffective management of the change process.

The capabilities that underpin successful corporate change programs in Australia are outlined by Turner in Chapter 9. The message is quite simple. To be effective in achieving change, management must achieve three things:

1 the *engagement* of the stakeholders in the firm;
2 the *development* of the firm's resources to meet the needs of the change; and
3 the simultaneous *performance management* of both the change process and the firm's ongoing operations.

This theme of change management is picked up in Chapter 10 by Sauer who illustrates the pervasive impact of underlying strategy paradigms on the development and implementation of IT management.

Sauer argues for an incremental approach to change, adapting the organisation-building sustainable advantage in single steps. In adopting this approach we seek value-increasing changes, while limiting the risk to the current step—we are able to measure performance at each step. The concept of value-increasing increments is consistent with the idea of strategic options discussed by Smith and Twite in Chapter 12 on the relationship between finance and strategy. In a vein similar to that discussed by Devinney around the acquisition and development of knowledge within the organisation, the incremental approach also means that the firm builds on existing competencies, learning as it goes.

Relational view

Over the last decade there has also been an evolution in the perception of how firms compete from exclusively firm versus firm competition to include chain or network versus network. In other words, the 'firm' must be considered in the context of the other stakeholders in the value-creation network, including customers, suppliers, substitutors and complementors. The terms substitutors and complementors are taken from Brandenburger and Nalebuff.[5] They define your substitutors to be firms from whom your customers may purchase products or to whom your suppliers may sell their products and your complementors to be firms from whom your customers may purchase complementary products or to whom your suppliers may sell complementary products. Network-level competition also introduces the notion of 'cooperating to compete'. Firms that are good cooperators can be more effective competitors. Thus, counter-intuitively, as markets become more deregulated and competitive, the importance of cooperating increases.

Dyer and Singh[6] identify the potential sources of sustainable advantage from cooperation to include:

- investment in relation-specific assets;
- sharing knowledge;
- utilising complementary capabilities or resources; and
- lower transaction costs.

These issues are explored in Chapter 11 by Michael O'Keeffe and David Wilson who maintain that the issue for management seeking to build sustainable advantage has become one of managing the boundaries of the firm—identifying the value-creation network. O'Keeffe and Wilson illustrate value-creating networks using the example of the impact of the development of the Internet and e-commerce on customer and supplier relationships. They contend that in this new environment firms must start defining their own value-creating network.

The alternatives

The relationship between these alternative views regarding sources of sustainable advantage is summarised in Table 1.1. The table seeks

Table 1.1 Alternative views of sustainable advantage

	Industry view	Resource-based view	Relational view
Unit of analysis	Industry	Firm	Network or value chain
Main influence on performance	Industry attractiveness	Firm's resources and competencies	Network configuration and competitiveness
Key task of managers	Choice of industry and position within industry	Create and nurture capabilities	Build alliances and leverage resources
Manager as	Portfolio builder	Capability builder	Cooperator and negotiator
Strategic degrees of freedom	Unlimited	Constrained by past investment decisions and future capabilities	Constrained by position in network
Response to environment	Adaptation and respond to change	Rejuvenation of capabilities and influence future environment	Manage and reconfigure the network

to compare the unit of analysis, performance, managerial roles and responses under the three alternatives views of sustainable advantage: (1) industry view, (2) resource-based view and (3) relational view.[7]

All three approaches seek to identify the source of sustainable competitive advantage to the firm and would agree that it is represented by an 'asset' unique to the firm. However, they differ on the question of where this 'asset' resides. The industry-based view would argue that sustainable competitive advantage stems from both the industry structure and the firm's position within the industry. While both the resource-based and relational views would argue that sustainable competitive advantage stems from assets or resources unique to the firm, the resource-based view argues that these resources reside within the firm. Alternatively, the relational view argues that they reside within the relationships that the firm has with its various stakeholders—suppliers, customers, substitutors and complementors.

While we can think of a firm's ability to manage its relationship with stakeholders as a firm-specific resource, it is worth distinguishing between a resource-based view and a relational-based view of the firm. While these two views differ in the source of sustainable advantage—firm-specific assets versus relation-specific assets—the important difference is the variable to be managed—firm versus network (or value chain).

The implication of this transition to firm resource has meant that the tools for analysing the firm are not well developed. Remember that the 1980s was dominated by an economic paradigm that viewed industry as the unit of analysis and there were well developed industry analysis frameworks of which Porter's Five-Forces model is the most well known. On the other hand, we are just starting to come to grips with the tools for assessing capabilities and resources at a firm level.

VALUATION

If we start by recognising that the outcome of sustainable advantage is value creation then the tools for assessing capabilities and resources must build upon the valuation tools which underpin finance.

Chapter 12 by Smith and Twite identifies the basic tools of valuation and asks how these three ideas of:

1 time value of money;
2 diversification; and
3 arbitrage

can be used to value strategic opportunities. The answer to this question lies in the realisation that strategic opportunities are like options and the finance literature has the tools to identify and value options. Smith and Twite identify the strategic options that firms may hold:

- flexibilty option held by management to revise operating decisions in response to market conditions;
- the option to wait before investing;
- the option to make follow-on investments if the immediate investment project succeeds; and
- the option to abandon the investment project.

These options describe the decisions faced by management in building sustainable advantage.

MANAGEMENT IMPLICATIONS

The shift in emphasis from 'industry' to 'firm' as the main driver of profitability has resulted in four important implications for management:

1 build sustainable advantage;
2 assess added value at each stage;
3 focus beyond the firm; and
4 maintain flexibility.

Management must recognise that sustainable advantage is built not brought. The current view states that if you can buy it—or it is tradeable—it can be replicated by others, hence, it is unlikely to lead to a sustainable competitive advantage. Core capabilities are built, not bought.

In building sustainable advantage management should focus on small, rather than big, decisions. The process of building sustainable advantage should be undertaken incrementally—building on existing competencies. Management will assess the value added by each decision. In adopting this approach we seek value-increasing changes, while limiting the risk to the current step.

In seeking to establish a sustainable competitive advantage, management should look beyond the firm's boundaries, don't ignore other stakeholders—customers, suppliers, substitutors and complementors. Management shouldn't just focus on resources idiosyncratic to the firm. We must recognise that sustainable competitive advantage can also arise through cooperation. The implication for management is to look beyond the firm's boundaries to the firm's network as a source of profitability.

Finally, management should seek to maintain flexibility. Competitive advantage is a fragile construct, it must be maintained. The creation and defence of sustainable advantage is a dynamic process, suggestive of a process of corporate change. The key to change is flexibility; it is operating flexibility that enables the firm to change in response to changing market conditions.

2

Competition policy: underlying ideas and issues

FREDERICK HILMER

Competition policy has struck a cord with politicians and the business and wider community far beyond anything my colleagues Mark Rayner and Geoff Taperell might have expected when we were asked by the Commonwealth Government to carry out an independent inquiry into the subject in late 1992. Competition policy, often expressed, albeit somewhat incorrectly, as shorthand for 'more competition', is now the central plank of reform in areas as diverse as electricity generation, legal services, health care and ports. This heightened interest in competition is not solely an Australian preoccupation. In Europe the European Commission is increasingly involved in a wide range of economic reform within the member states of the European Economic Community, including utilities reform and the appropriateness of state subsidies. In the US competition policy is being applied not merely through traditional anti-trust enforcement but in new proposals such as for the creation of a market in electricity and for the restructuring of that industry.

Competition policy is however a term that can cover a wide range of policies, and that reflects a large number of economic concepts, some relatively soundly established and some largely speculative. The purpose of this chapter is to look behind the political rhetoric, lay out what is meant by competition policy, and discuss some of the main underlying ideas and issues in the field. The discussion is intended to provide a better appreciation of the subject to those likely to be affected by the application of competition policy. Without this understanding businesses are likely to be swept along by the tide of reforms rather than constructively contribute to shaping and adapting the field.

WHAT IS COMPETITION POLICY?

Early in the National Competition Policy Committee's deliberations the view was expressed that the main element of competition policy was Part IV of the *Trade Practices Act* (TPA) covering anti-competitive behaviours such as price fixing, boycotts or mergers that severely limited competition in a market. The central issue for national policy, it was argued, was whether and how to extend this law to the many sectors of the economy not then covered by Part IV. For a variety of reasons, some due to constitutional limitations and some due to the way the law was written, the TPA had limited application to public utilities such as electricity, gas, transport and communications, the professions and agricultural marketing. Part IV of the TPA is similar to overseas competition legislation such as the US anti-trust laws, the UK's Restrictive Practices Act, the Canadian Competition Act and the European Community's Treaty of Rome, Articles 85 and 86, though these laws are not limited in terms of areas of application to the same extent as the Australian Law. Competition laws such as Part IV seek to protect the competitive process by:

- Regulating actions of firms that might significantly reduce competition without offsetting benefits, such as mergers, acquisitions and agreements between competitors. Regulation ranges from outright prohibition of certain conduct such as price fixing to the requirement for approval of arrangements by a competition regulator.

- Restricting firms with significant market power from using their power to harm the process of competition in a market, for example by refusing to supply an intermediate product or service to a competitor in a market.

However, it soon became apparent that regulating actions by and among firms via laws like Part IV was only one part of a much broader set of laws, policies and government actions that defined the nature and extent of competition in an economy. We found that in most cases the factors that either encouraged or limited competition were not the rules of the TPA but other regulations and market structures that resulted from the actions of governments in establishing and operating businesses over many years, and/or the direct actions of governments themselves. For example, applying the TPA would not affect agricultural marketing arrangements embodied in specific legislation. The reason was that producers who sold their products to a statutory authority with powers of compulsory acquisition at a fixed price were not price fixing but simply complying with direct legislation. Nor would applying the TPA lead to a more competitive structure for generation and transmission of electricity, place government businesses on an equal competitive footing with private businesses or deal with regulatory barriers to entry in many fields, such as prohibitions on carriage of certain freight by road or restrictions on the practice of conveyancing by those other than legal practitioners.

Against this background, and mindful of the second of our terms of reference,[1] the Committee defined competition policy to include six main elements, as set out in Table 2.1.

Our first proposal was for the universal application of the conduct rules in the TPA to all business activities, irrespective of legal form or ownership. Despite the fact that universal application of the rules would not in and of itself be sufficient as a competition policy, extending these rules was an important signal of the kind of behaviour that was required in competitive markets and a way to stop or prevent conduct that most sectors now accepted as not permissible. Key findings with respect to the other five elements of competition policy are set out below.

Table 2.1 Elements of competition policy

Policy element	Example
1 Limiting anti-competitive conduct of firms	Competitive conduct rules such as those in Part IV of the *Trade Practices Act*
2 Reforming regulation which unjustifiably restricts competition	Deregulation of domestic aviation, egg marketing and telecommunications
3 Reforming the structure of public monopolies to facilitate competition	Proposed restructuring of energy utilities in several states
4 Providing third-party access to certain facilities that are essential for competition	Access arrangements for the telecommunications network
5 Restraining monopoly pricing behaviour	Prices surveillance by Prices Surveillance Authority
6 Fostering 'competitive neutrality' between government and private businesses when they compete	Requirements for government businesses to make tax-equivalent payments

Source: *National Competition Policy*, Report by the Independent Committee of Inquiry, (1993), p. xvii.

Regulatory restrictions on competition

The greatest impediment to enhance competition in many sectors of the economy are the restrictions imposed through government regulation—whether in the form of statutes or subordinate legislation—or government ownership.

Examples include legislated monopolies for public utilities, statutory marketing arrangements for many agricultural products and licensing arrangements for various occupations, businesses and professions.

Consequently we recommended that all Australian governments agree to principles and processes to review whether legislative restrictions on competition could be justified. This review process began with the creation of the National Competition Council and the Australian Competition and Consumer Commission.

Structural reform of public monopolies

The removal of regulatory restrictions on competition may not be sufficient to foster effective competition in sectors currently dominated by public monopolies. Work by the OECD has highlighted the importance of creating competitive market and industry structures if effective competition is to emerge.[2] Three principles were put forward, and have now been accepted. These are:

1 the separation of regulatory and commercial functions of public monopolies;
2 the separation of natural monopoly and potentially competitive activities;
3 the separation of potentially competitive activities into a number of smaller, independent competing business units.

Access to essential facilities

Introducing competition in some markets requires that competitors be assured of access to certain facilities that cannot be duplicated economically—referred to as 'essential facilities'. Effective competition in electricity generation and rail services, for example, will require firms to have access to the electricity transmission grid and rail tracks.

While the misuse of the market power provision of the TPA can sometimes apply in these situations, submissions to this Inquiry confirmed the Committee's own assessment that something more is required to meet the needs of an effective competition policy.

The Committee recommended that a new legal regime be established under which firms could in certain circumstances be given a right of access to specified 'essential facilities' on fair and reasonable terms. This has been done, though the access regimes are somewhat more complex than envisaged in our report.

Monopoly pricing

Where the conditions for effective competition are absent—such as where firms have a legislated or natural monopoly or the market is otherwise poorly contestable—firms may be able to charge prices above efficient levels for periods beyond a time when a competitive response might reasonably be expected. Such 'monopoly pricing' is detrimental to consumers and to the community as a whole. The TPA does not address this issue, and the *Price Surveillance Act* has a limited reach.

The Committee considered the primary response of competition policy in these markets should be to increase competitive pressures, including by removing regulatory restrictions, restructuring public monopolies and, if need be, providing third-party access rights. Where measures of this kind are not practical or sufficient, some form of price-based response may be appropriate.

The Committee accordingly recommended that a national competition policy should include a carefully targeted prices monitoring and surveillance process to apply in such cases.

Competitive neutrality

Moves to increase the efficiency of government businesses through commercialisation and the introduction of competition have raised a new set of issues for competition policy, particularly where those businesses continue to enjoy net advantages vis-a-vis private competitors. As competition of this kind is likely to increase over the next decade, there is a growing need to find some mechanism to deal with 'competitive neutrality' concerns.

The Committee recommended that Commonwealth, State and Territory Governments adopt a set of principles aimed at ensuring government-owned businesses comply with certain competitive neutrality requirements when competing with private firms.

In defining competition policy this way we were explicitly recognising that competition policy was not about the pursuit of competition as an end in itself. Clearly, the Committee viewed competition as an important and powerful force for economic efficiency and concluded that economic efficiency generally was of great benefit to consumers. The recommended processes have a presumption in favour of competition, and place the onus of arguing for suspension of competition on those who seek exemptions or special treatment. However, we recognised that competition might not always be effective in achieving consumer benefits or that it might lead to conflicts with other social goals. Competition policy thus aims to produce guidelines that determine the nature and extent of competition and the ways in which possible conflicts between the results of competition, economic efficiency and other social goals are to be handled.

UNDERLYING IDEAS AND ISSUES

The Committee's starting point was to accept the notion that in most cases competition will produce economic efficiency, and that economic efficiency generally enhances consumer welfare. The submission from Commonwealth Treasury described the role of competition in promoting three types of efficiency in the terms listed below.

1. Technical or productive efficiency is achieved where individual firms produce the goods and services that they offer to consumers at *least cost*. Competition can enhance technical efficiency by, for example, stimulating improvements in managerial performance, work practices, and the use of material inputs.
2. Allocative efficiency is achieved where resources used to produce a set of goods or services are allocated to their highest valued uses (i.e. those that provide the greatest benefit relative to costs). Competition tends to increase allocative efficiency, because firms that can use particular resources more productively can afford to bid those resources away from firms that cannot achieve the same level of returns.
3. Dynamic efficiency reflects the need for industries to make timely changes to technology and products in response to changes in consumer tastes and in productive opportunities. Competition in markets for goods and services provides incentives to undertake research and development, effect innovation in product design, reform management structures and strategies and create new products and production processes.

The interesting issues in competition policy are not however about these general linkages between competition and efficiency. Economics has been comfortable with these sorts of generalisations for hundreds of years. Rather the interesting issues that are emerging as the six elements of competition policy are being implemented are about the nature and extent of competition that is required to produce these results, and the effect and appropriateness of different regulatory models, for example, with respect to access pricing or other price controls. A number of issues are also being raised with respect to the impact of competition on other social goals.

Each of these subjects will be discussed in turn.

Effective competition

The requirements of effective or workable competition, that is, competition that is likely to produce economic efficiency, is a difficult but central question in competition policy. Competition regulators continually face this question, for example, when ruling on whether a merger ought to be prohibited because it significantly limits competition without offsetting benefits. Similarly, in administering the other elements of competition policy, answers to questions of how many competitors are 'enough', whether the threat of a new entrants is adequate to produce competitive outcomes or whether regulations that limit market entry or determine pricing structures can be justified, depend on the view taken with respect to effective competition.

In his autobiography, *Memoirs of An Unregulated Economist*,[3] George Stigler reviewed how economic thinking had shifted from the view that competition was a 'delicate flower', requiring large numbers of small firms competing head to head, to the view that in fact it was a 'tough weed'. Being a 'tough weed' meant that competition seems to work even when there are few participants in a market and where the leading participant has quite a high market share, or enjoys some regulatory protections such as licensing.

Stigler based this conclusion on both empirical studies and economic theory. Some of the key studies were those of underwriters bidding in the bond market for the right to raise funds at a price, called spread, paid by the issuing entity. When, say, twenty groups of underwriters (clearly a large number of competitors) were bidding, the spread on price to the issuer was $14 per $1000 bond. When only one group bid the spread was $20, implying a monopoly profit of $6. However when two bidders were involved, the spread dropped to $17 and with three bidders it fell to $16. Other evidence from the oil and steel industries found similar results, suggesting that the benefits of competition are produced by relatively few competitors.

In terms of theory, Stigler relied on a number of ideas. Schumpeter's arguments were clearly influential as the following quote illustrates:

> The competition which counts is from the new commodity, the new technology, the new source of supply, the new type of organisation . . . competition which strikes not at the margins of profits and outputs of the existing firms but at their foundations and their very lives.[4]

Schumpeter would define markets broadly, and expect competition between segments as well as within them.

Stigler also relied on classical economic theory which suggested that even with a few competitors there was a strong incentive for an individual firm to discount if prices were above competitive levels, and that such discounting would be difficult to detect. The incentive to discount would be stronger if the item produced could not be stored, as is usually the case with services, or if perishable goods were being produced. Hence conspiracies to raise prices would tend to be hard to form and unstable.

Despite Stigler's confidence that competition is a strong weed, and that a little competition produces most of the efficiency benefits, the debate about the requirements for effective competition continues, and new tools, especially modelling, are being used in an effort to throw more light on the subject. One market where numerous studies are under way, and where opinions remain divided, is the market for electricity generation. The electricity industry has become a key candidate for the application of competition policy in many economies. Once considered a single industry with many so-called natural monopoly features, the electricity industry is now being restructured, with the separation of monopoly components, particularly transmission and distribution, from potentially competitive components, most notably generation. Australia, Britain, Scandinavia and other parts of Europe and the US now recognise that if transmission is operated as a common carrier providing non-discriminatory service, then generators can compete for customers via a combination of spot, forward and long-term contracts.

The UK market has been most studied and modelled, but debate is heating up in the US, particularly California, and there has been considerable analysis of the Australian market, including the Industry Commission[5] and London Economics.[6] Studies have covered both the numbers of competitors required for effective competition, as well as the rules that determine how prices are set overall and for each supplier. For example, Green and Newbery[7] modelled what they described as an effective duopoly in the UK, and on the basis of this explained why prices were considerably above marginal cost as well as why excessive entry of new gas generators was occurring. Their model suggested that had the two generators been divided into five roughly equivalent-sized firms, most of the excessive social costs could have been avoided.

Von der Fehr and Harbord[8] focused on the price setting rules rather than the structure, and found these too were critical. They found that an auction system where the price received by a generator was independent of its own bid was more likely to induce marginal cost bidding than when each generator set called into operation received the specific price it had bid.

A similar kind of analysis was carried out by London Economics for the Industry Commission to assist the NSW Generation Review Group to determine the desirable restructuring for Pacific Power. Pacific Power once held about 90 per cent of the NSW market for power. With a four-state east coast market in operation, its share would be about 36 per cent. The modelling was fairly simple in concept. Each participant in the market was able to make one of three bids each half hour—marginal cost, two-times marginal cost or three-times marginal cost. The mix of bids that produced a stable Nash equilibrium—that is, where any participant who bid differently would earn a lower profit—was selected. If price was found to be above marginal cost the outcome was labelled non-competitive. The market was modelled with five to eleven groups of generators bidding independently. Interestingly, the simulation found that disaggregating Pacific Power into two groups (that is, a market with a minimum of six independent bidders) did not change prices much and that a split into three groups lowered price somewhat (about one-third of the time), but that prices still tended to be above marginal costs. In summary, the electricity studies, unlike the earlier work relied on by Stigler, are concluding that quite a large number of competitors are required to achieve efficiency.[9]

Such studies however raise a number of important and difficult questions such as those that follow.

- Whether pricing above marginal cost is in fact evidence of poor resource allocation and lack of competition. How can profit be explained in this view of the world? Why would a firm invest if the day after capacity came on stream and a shortage of capacity no longer existed, no return on investment and only marginal costs could be recouped in prices. Work in the US[10] has questioned the validity of marginal cost pricing as a test of competitiveness, recognising that even in competitive markets firms seek to earn a return on sunk costs. Hence the higher the sunk costs, the higher the expected prices.
- Whether the results in electricity are better explained by 'folk theorems' whereby, given the high quality and quantity of public information in firm performance and the similarity of firms, an outcome that appears collusive occurs without collusion. This raises the question whether competition is sufficient to ensure competitive prices in these kinds of markets, and if not, what else is needed by way of process or regulation.
- Whether more complex and richer models using game theory will produce better insights. For example:
  - Whether modelling can better take account of shocks and thus consider the option value in some cases of waiting, holding back investment, and in others of preempting competitors by investing when there is still unused capacity in the industry.[11]
  - Whether modelling based on market value of the firm rather than period profit leads to different outcomes. A firm's value will depend only to a small extent on profit at a particular time. Expected future earnings and options available to the firm as well as the riskiness of the earnings will be more important. Whether modellers are able to take this set of factors into account is not yet clear.
  - Recognising that firms have both memories and the capacity to project courses of action and that there are various views of 'rationality' possible rather than looking at equilibria in short periods of time, whether modelling is able to consider different equilibria in present value terms if

various pathways are followed by players with different goals.[12]

- Whether more recent empirical work using modern computational and statistical techniques to carry out studies similar to those referred to by Stigler earlier would confirm what the models suggest?

Because of these kind of limitations, modelling plays little role in corporate strategy, and was given relatively little weight in the policy work on electricity. While modelling can be improved and undoubtedly will consume countless hours of doctoral and post-doctoral research, it would be disappointing if preoccupation with techniques caused researchers to lose sight of the key question; namely, whether, to use Stigler's words, competition is a fragile flower or a tough weed.

Regulatory models

Even if competition is a tough weed, there are times when effective competition is not practical. There are two such situations under the National Competition Policy, as administered by the National Competition Council. The first is where an essential facility with natural monopoly characteristics exists and competitors require access to the facility. The second is where a firm has significant market power that cannot be dealt with by other means such as removing regulatory barriers to competition or changing market structure and thus price surveillance may be warranted. Both these situations raise quite difficult practical and theoretical problems. In each case regulation creates a set of incentives that in turn drive behaviour in the regulated firm and also that of customers and suppliers. This stream of behaviours is often difficult to predict, and often surprises regulators by producing unintended and costly results.

Access regimes

Facilities where access is seen as important include the local telecommunications network, the electricity grid and certain gas pipelines. The interesting economic question is the process and basis for setting access prices. The National Competition Policy report, after reviewing the literature, concluded that there was no one best or correct way to do this, and that at this stage a case-by-case approach was appropriate. Under this approach the relevant minister would first outline the pricing principles. Parties would then negotiate and if necessary arbitrate price in accordance with the principles.

The access pricing problem is more difficult when the firm owning the essential facility, and thus providing the access, also competes in the end-use market. This is common in telecommunications when one supplier owns local, long distance and mobile networks and competitors are involved only in long distance and/or mobile services. In these cases the owner of the essential facility (the local network) has an incentive to use its monopoly position in the local network to drive out competition in the potentially competitive long distance and mobile services. The same situation can exist where an electricity utility owns both high voltage transmission and generation. Our first preference was to recommend structural separation of essential facilities from potentially competitive activities. Once separation is achieved, the operator of the essential facility has the incentive to provide access to whoever wishes to use the facility in order to maximise the returns from the facility. In these cases, price control may be unnecessary, or quite 'light handed'.

Where price control is needed, particularly in cases where separation is not possible, a number of different pricing approaches have been suggested including:[13]

- short run marginal cost pricing; that is, prices to recover only the increase in direct operating or cash costs due to an increase in use of the facility;
- long run marginal cost pricing; that is, pricing that includes a cost for all factors of production including capital ownership and replacement;
- average cost; that is, pricing all output at the average price even when average costs might decrease with increasing output;
- Ramsay pricing; that is, charging different prices to different types of customer who have different price elasticities and cannot on-sell to each other;
- efficient component pricing (Baumol-Willig Rule); that is, price

to include the opportunity cost borne by the access provider as well as average marginal costs;
- non-linear (for example, two-part) tariffs.

The appropriateness of each rule differs depending on factors such as capacity utilisation of the facility, technology, information availability and variability of demand. Also, some rules will be more pro-competitive than others, so that a government wishing to encourage competition in a sector might argue for marginal cost pricing, while if capacity is constrained or expensive, efficient component pricing could be advocated. Consequently, we recommended that in each case the first step was for the relevant minister to determine the principles that would govern access pricing and then for the parties to negotiate in light of these principles.

Negotiations in the context of principles would overcome problems such as those raised by King.[14] King suggests that negotiating parties who are not obliged to comply with any pricing principles would have an incentive to structure an arrangement that creates a monopoly in the final goods market; for example, via two-tier pricing with a fixed fee and variable component related to volume. In this case the high market share company in the end-user market would be able to split a monopoly price with the access provider. These kinds of concerns imply a 'delicate flower' view of competition that leads to a greater degree of regulation of access pricing than if the 'tough weed' approach was followed.

Pricing controls

A second area of regulation that is receiving increasing attention is price controls. In our review of this field we identified a number of approaches currently being used. These are summarised in Table 2.2.

Again, as with access pricing, these rules will work differently in different situations of capacity, technology, information availability and variability of demand. Experience is suggesting that all these pricing rules have problems in terms of unintended and undesirable consequences such as over-investment with rate of return rules or inefficiencies with cost-plus pricing. Even CPI-X rules run into difficulties when, as in telecommunications, the industry has enormous opportunities available to increase efficiency

Table 2.2 Examples of possible pricing approaches

Approach	Elements	Comments
Cost-based	Price changes linked to changes in firm's costs	• Flexible as to changes in costs • Limited incentives to improve efficiency
Price (or revenue) capping ('CPI-X')	Price (or revenue) changes linked to a set rate ('X') below (usually) increases in the Consumer Price Index	• Clear benefits to consumers • Incentive to improve efficiency (particularly if X is set for reasonably lengthy periods) • Allows firms to restructure prices
Yardstick	Price changes linked to average (or lowest) changes in costs of a group of peer firms	• Incentives to improve efficiency • Eliminates need to determine X • Most effective when firms are readily comparable
Return-based	Price changes set in a context of firm earning set rate of return on investment	• Incentive to invest, meet market needs • Potentially very complex • Limited incentive to improve efficiency or avoid unnecessary investment

and provide new value-added services. Research is also showing that some pricing rules, for example, those designed to limit variability as in agricultural marketing schemes, can cause average prices to increase.[15]

Again, as with access, both empirical study of pricing approaches as well as modelling and simulation are likely to help the thinking through of consequences of different types of pricing regulation. Research may also demonstrate more sharply that the costs of regulation are high in terms of lost investment and/or inefficiency, and that it remains preferable to allow monopoly pricing in the short and medium term to attract entry of new or different forms of competition.

SOCIAL GOALS

The preceding sections examined some economic issues underlying competition policy. However there are also non-economic considerations that arise when government seeks to introduce and apply competition policy. This is because while competition may deliver greater efficiency, it may do so in a manner that is unacceptable to an electorate. Such situations typically involve universal access at prices that are widely affordable to what are seen as essential services. For example, access to water, power and phone services are seen as almost a 'right' of every citizen. More recently, there has been heated political debate about whether a basic banking service at a low or zero fee is not also in this category. Yet, because competition is intolerant of cross subsidies and usually requires users to pay fees that cover service costs, some people or groups, for example, rural consumers, may not be able to afford a service as priced by a market. A related situation exists when the electorate could afford to pay a market-based price but simply doesn't want to, as is the case with timed local calls.

There are economic explanations for this behaviour, most notably public choice theory. However, explaining the behaviour in terms of economic theory or exhorting governments not to be political might be intellectually rewarding but is of little impact. Meanwhile, implicit cross subsidies via uneconomic pricing practices continue. Our work on competition policy suggested that the cost of achieving social goals via the price structure was higher than necessary. However, we saw no empirical work that focused on the effectiveness of different types of distribution mechanisms as opposed to assertions that redistributions or cross subsidies were costly and should be made more transparent.

Consequently, a constructive line of research might be to explore ways in which these social goals of redistribution can be achieved with less economic cost due to market distortion or incentives to waste resources. The most common answer to this problem is to:

- make the redistribution transparent; that is, don't bury a cross subsidy in the accounts of the service provider but explicitly show the extra costs and thus diverted revenue of serving groups at below cost;
- ensure that the redistribution is paid for either by an allocation of government funds or via a levy or tax that is imposed in ways that do not distort markets, or by providing the intended beneficiary with a voucher or money; that is, always avoid cross subsidies in the pricing structure of the producer.

These approaches have limitations. First, they can be quite difficult to apply, and the approaches themselves are open to the possibility of abuse. For example, when is a cross subsidy in fact not a cross subsidy or social payment but rather a useful form of Ramsay pricing, or a way to build demand and goodwill among a user group that will be able to afford higher prices over time? Discounts to this end exist in commercial markets. Second, while aggregate costs for cross subsidy may be possible to calculate, the effect on various groups or subgroups might be hard to compute. Moreover, the incentive for providers of such services to overstate costs, especially where costs are shared, and/or difficult to verify, is high.

The main political stumbling block to more widespread application of competition policy is community concern about how these social goals will be achieved, and discomfort with ways in which the solutions of transparency and direct funding are being applied. Hence research both to better understand the impact of different mechanisms and to find new and better ways to achieve these goals would be of high practical value, even if it is not at the cutting edge of contemporary economic theory.

In short, many of the areas of competition policy are not amenable to simple answers based on the application of proven principles. The economic logic on which competition policy is based is still being formulated. Academic reviews of the effectiveness of anti-trusts are at best equivocal.[16] The application of economic theories to issues such as access to so-called essential facilities produces much learned though conflicting expert evidence, as seen in the New Zealand case of Clear Communications.[17] Economic theory is also quite unclear with respect to the relative weight to be given to domestic versus international competition.[18]

Nor are there well-established moral principles on which a community can rely to determine when commercial activity ought be considered 'wrong'. Is it 'wrong' for Nike's management to seek to energise their staff by adopting the slogan 'crush Reebok'? Is it 'wrong' for a group of farmers to seek a regulated cooperative marketing scheme for their products? What each of these examples illustrates is that what is at issue is more often a trade-off between the interests of groups—Nike versus Reebok, the owner of the pipeline and the community that would like others to find and pipe in competing gas, or the farmers and their customers. Put another way, to quote from the *Economist*, competition regulation involves 'a great deal of art as well as science',[19] as these competing claims need to be weighed and balanced.

As competition policy becomes more developed and entrenched not only in Australia but in most developed economies, business people will need to understand the principles and issues. Otherwise, they risk being unable to anticipate where and how their operations might be affected. More importantly, without a sound knowledge of the field, businesses will be ineffective in arguing their case and shaping what is likely to be a continually evolving field.

FURTHER READING

National Competition Policy. Report by the Independent Committee of Inquiry, AGPS, Canberra, 1993.
A full explanation of the basis for current competition policy in Australia.

OECD, *Regulatory Reform, Privatisation and Competition Policy*, 1992.
An overview of developments in the OECD.

George J. Stigler, *Memoirs of an Unregulated Economist*, Basic Books, Inc., New York, 1988.
A readable account of economic issues relevant to competition.

Avinash K. Dixit and Robert S. Pindyck, *Investment Under Uncertainty*, Princeton University Press, Princeton, NJ, 1993.
A game theory analysis of competitive behaviour.

Colin F. Camerer, 'Does Strategy Research Need Game Theory?', in *Fundamental Issues in Strategy*, edited by Richard P. Rumelt, Dan E. Schendel and David J. Teece, Harvard Business School Press, Boston, 1994.
A critique of game theory as a practical tool in strategy.

P. Yetton, J. Craig, J. Davis and F. Hilmer, 'Are Diamonds a Country's Best Friend? A Critique of Porter's Theory of National Competition as Applied to Canada, New Zealand and Australia', *Australian Journal of Management*, 17, 1, June 1992, pp. 89–120.
An overview of the application of strategic ideas to industry policy in Australia, Canada and New Zealand.

3

Business strategy and industry policy

IAN MARSH

Can the state contribute to business success? Current conventional wisdom answers largely in the negative. Policy making and political elites both discount state action in favour of a predominant role for market forces. The theory that lies behind this approach concerns efficient resource allocation. According to this theory, market choice is invariably a superior allocation system to political choice. In a market, business people are hazarding their own assets and pursuing their own interests. Consumers are expressing their own tastes and preferences and spending their own money. The prices thus established embody this intelligence. They are the best guides to choice. By contrast, the incentives facing politicians and bureaucrats work in the opposite direction. In the words of some academic sceptics: 'Misapplication, abuse, interest group capture, mistaken targeting and bungling can bring about economically undesirable outcomes'.

There is of course some truth in the conventional wisdom. Yet there are also current examples of successful government–industry partnerships. How, for example, can the spectacular success of the Australian wine industry be explained? Through its elaborated collaborative arrangements, this industry has produced a shared vision of its long-term future. This bases industry development on international expansion. In turn, this is to result from linkage of brand development, innovation and a move to premium market segments. Implementation has required partnership with state and federal governments in regulation, governance, research and training. Government roles in other emerging clusters remain considerable. For example, an indigenous IT industry will not emerge without government action. Biotechnology is also heavily dependent on state initiatives. The Prime Minister's appointment of an investment advisor points to a state role in attracting large scale foreign direct investment.

Whereas the conventional wisdom of the 1980s was almost wholly hostile to an active government role, recent scholarly research provides the basis for a more nuanced perspective. Developments in the disciplines of economics and business strategy are one source. Despite the financial crisis, another source is studies of the actual practices of Japan and the East Asian 'Tigers'. A third is studies of the varieties of capitalism. There is no capitalism with a big C, rather there are a variety of small c patterns.

THE ROLE OF INSTITUTIONS

Perhaps the strongest attack on current conventional wisdom comes from the 'new institutionalists'. According to a leading exponent of this approach, Douglass North, a Nobel prize winner in economics, 'we have paid a big price for the uncritical acceptance of neo-classical theory'.[1] North argues the neoclassical model of allocation is too simplified to be an exclusive guide to policy. There are two fundamental problems. First, its model of choice is totally unrealistic in its assumptions about available information and about choice. Second, transaction and coordination costs, not transformation costs, are the decisive long-run determinants of growth and of economic performance. Transaction costs are ineradicable in an uncertain world. These are simply assumed away in the frictionless neoclassical model.

Yet the twin contemporary imperatives of innovation-led development and economic globalisation make these variables especially significant for economic performance.

The noted business strategy scholar John Dunning argues economic growth is increasingly based on two sources—innovation and participation in the global economy. Both these sources of growth give institutions, such as government policies and practices, a new salience. This is because institutions determine the incentive or disincentive effects of transaction and coordination costs.[2]

Innovation and participation in the global economy both raise the salience of transaction and coordination costs at the cluster or sectoral level. For example, innovation places new emphasis on the linkage between research in its various phases and firms. The potential disjunction between social costs and benefits, cluster costs and benefits and firm level costs have been widely recognised. Institutions determine whether systemic and other opportunities are fully exploited, whether the social externalities of markets for dynamic goods are fully realised and whether 'the social assets necessary for the efficient upgrading and exploitation of the core competencies of firms and industries are adequately provided'.

Similarly, economic globalisation enhances the significance of spatially-related coordination and transaction costs. These increase as markets become more uncertain and volatile, more specialised, complex and interdependent, or characterised by externalities, information asymmetries and opportunism. All of these conditions are significantly enhanced by globalisation. The impact of these costs is determined by institutions.

Further, Dunning argues the withdrawal of the state from many operational roles in the 1980s has been matched by the need to enhance its effectiveness in systemic roles. This is partly because of the general or societal transaction and coordination costs caused by whole systems (for example, the tax, education or research systems). It is also partly because of the need (and potential) for strategic leadership in opinion formation. To quote Dunning:

> One of the consequences of globalisation is to underscore the role of national governments as vision-setters and institution-builders; as ensurers of the availability of high quality, locationally bound inputs; as smoothers of the course of economic change; and as creators of the

right ethos for entrepreneurship, innovation, learning, and high quality standards.[3]

This shifts attention from the immediate cluster environment to the broader political institutional matrix. Here institutions constitute the *mise en scene* for the engagement of political parties, the bureaucracy, business associations, trade unions, environmentalists and others. In the process, they frame opinion formation for the broader society.

Douglass North follows this theme in his discussion of the impact of institutions on the 'ideas, choice sets and motives' of relevant organisations and individuals.[4] In the process, he challenges neoclassical assumptions concerning preference formation, the decision calculus, and the availability and assimilation of information.

Drawing on recent cognitive literature, he argues choice is framed by mental models that are widely shared, that are established collectively, and that are inherently partial ('ideologies'); that using such models to interpret uncertain events compounds the hazards of judgment; that in such a context optimising, or even satisficing, does not necessarily produce positive outcomes; and finally that feedback is non corrective since this process is subject to the same uncertainties as initial judgments.[5]

Widely shared mental models are established collectively, by and through institutions. Their 'quality' thus becomes a critical element in competitiveness. Further, path dependence means particular historic decisions can maintain dysfunctional patterns of economic (or other) activity. This analysis suggests a wholly novel perspective from which the effectiveness of institutions might be judged, namely their contribution to opinion formation. This can occur at systemic or cluster levels.

In general, these theoretical perspectives suggest the need for a much more broadly-based approach to industry strategy both at cluster and systemic levels.

FIVE ELEMENTS OF A POSITIVE INDUSTRY STRATEGY

Theory and practice suggest a positive approach might have five key elements. First, a more strategic approach is needed in economic and industry policy. Economic and social strategy is currently defined by the annual budget cycle, or at best the three-year electoral cycle. The longer term in most public and media discussion is the next twelve months. Can we establish the broad terms of the kind of society and economy we would like to be in an eight to ten year perspective—the kind of vision development routinely undertaken by major corporations? The National Economic Summit in 1983 was a quasi-example. Can such a process be made routine?[6]

Second, what are some gaps in our national manufacturing and service portfolio? Can we identify the gaps? Can we establish strategies to fill them? For example, what is the condition of Australia's electronics and IT clusters—these are the fastest growing sectors in world trade and the key drivers of current US economic performance. Despite present difficulties, Korea built a presence at the cutting edge of chip manufacture in the absence of any of the elements of Michael Porter's 'diamond of competitive advantage'.[7] Korea succeeded without any prime mover advantage. Fashionable theories need to be tested against experience.

Can we establish and implement sectoral or cluster strategies—for sectors that are emerging, that are in the high growth segments, or that offer high value jobs? For example, autos and auto parts, design and construction, financial services, education and health. We have tried with pharmaceuticals, tourism, agrifoods and various commodities. What are the lessons of this experience? In all these cases markets led, and governments followed. Governments were not, as antagonists falsely assert, picking winners. They were rather following, and trying to optimise, market-created opportunities.

Third, Ireland, Wales, Scotland, Singapore and most of Southeast Asia show the benefits of a deliberate strategy to attract multinational corporations (MNCs). MNCs are playing an increasingly significant role in world trade.[8] The proportion of trade that is intra-firm, and foreign direct investment (FDI) itself, are both growing at three or four times the rate of increase of world exports, output or GDP. Technology and other factors are unbundling the value chain within MNCs and creating opportunities for states to define and project their distinctive comparative advantages.[9] Ireland and Singapore have built major industry segments in electronics and financial services by a determined effort to attract MNCs. They then put in place arrangements to ensure linkages to local firms and workers through schemes covering procurement, skills development and technology transfer. The philosophies and policies of the Irish Industry Development Authority and the Singapore Economic Development Board are a far cry from their Australian counterparts.[10]

Fourth, how can we establish business–government collaboration to sustain such approaches? Australia has a thoroughly developed pattern of industry associations. They have played key brokerage roles historically in relation to industrial relations. Can they play new brokerage roles, for example, in relation to sectoral or cluster development, skills, innovation, networking and so forth? Collaboration is a two-way affair. Existing approaches to consultation between the state and private interests are often a sham, with submissions invited but with decisions made in private by officials and ministers. Can more fruitful and productive interchanges be established?

Finally, where are the elite bureaucrats who might design such collaborative approaches? The Treasury line has so dominated public policy that it is unclear if sufficient uncommitted bureaucrats remain to design and implement necessary frameworks. At the least, an intellectual capacity would need to be developed in the public service—as the old Tariff Board and Industry Commission nourished a similar development earlier, but in the reverse direction.

Thinking about alternative approaches now exists only on the margins of Australian public policy. Elite opinion is so formed and key political leaders so committed that change will perhaps require a slide in the electoral fortunes of the major parties. Whatever the political circumstances, a radically alternative framework is available. This could guide the design of public policy to nourish business success. Relations between business firms and the state would need to be recast. But an amplified and more finely grained conception of the role of the state promises to optimise business success, strengthen national competitiveness and preserve the aspiration for fairness Australians have traditionally valued.

FURTHER READING

J. Dunning (ed), *Governments, Globalisation and International Business*, Oxford University Press, Oxford, 1997; also, *Alliance Capitalism and Global Business*, Routledge, London, 1997.
This book provides a comprehensive, accessible overview of key contemporary developments: economic globalisation, developments in various branches of theory, the changing roles of the state and business and the emerging role of the state.

M. Porter, 'Clusters and the New Economics of Competition', *Harvard Business Review*, November 1998, pp. 77–90.
This article is an accessible survey of the new role of clusters in thinking about economic capacities.

I. Marsh, *Beyond the Two Party System? Political Representation, Economic Competitiveness and Australian Politics*, Cambridge University Press, Melbourne, 1995.
This is a self-serving citation. But this book explores the possibility, and the institutional form, of the changes to political institutions that might be required to give the state a more strategic role in economic developments. It also explores the changing character of the Australian electorate.

4

The triumph of the firm

ROBERT MARKS[1]

Henri Szeps, the actor, is a neighbour of mine. As an actor he usually signs a contract which specifies a given amount of pay per performance; his income is certain, so long as the show goes on, but a sell-out audience makes no difference to his pay. Henri recently returned from a very successful run of his one-man show, *I Am Not A Dentist*, in Melbourne. Unusually, Henri is both the actor, the scriptwriter and the producer of this show. As such, he bears the risk of the show folding and he reaps the rewards of sell-out crowds, such as he enjoyed in Melbourne. We drank to his success.

As an actor, Henri is usually employed by the producer and submits to the director. His wage is reasonably insensitive to the box office take. The contract will usually specify a specific cast, performing at specific locations, for specific periods, for specific pay. But there is an alternative form of employment for stage actors. A repertory company will have longer-term contracts: the actors become employees of the company for the interim, taking whatever parts in whatever plays at whatever venues on whatever dates as management decrees. In the theatre, the short-term contract is the norm, while the repertory company contract—and the actor-producer—is unusual.

When we look beyond the theatre to industry at large, we see that the opposite is true and one sort of arrangement predominates. It exhibits long-term contracts with at least some of its suppliers, owners who direct employees lower in the hierarchy in production and who bear the risks of high or low returns, and a size of organisation which takes advantage of economies of scale, with the need for coordination at larger sizes. It is the firm.

What are the reasons for the existence of the firm? Why not the theatre's short-term arrangements? Over the past twenty years or more, economists have turned to asking questions about the meaning and purpose of the firm, and have come up with answers that have helped advance our understanding of the firm and its management. They have focused on organisational factors rather than the technological factors which have provided a rationale for the firm in standard micro-economic theory.

With downsizing and outsourcing, not to mention privatisation, there has been a recent focus of attention on the size and extent of the firm. Perhaps not coincidentally this interest has been accompanied by renewed involvement on the part of economic theorists on the economic theory of the firm, which previously had almost entirely been seen as a black box, the producing counterpart to the consuming household.

You may be asking, what have economic theorists ever done for the real world? Well, Maynard Keynes for one, in a celebrated passage in his *General Theory*, spoke of economic theorists in these terms:

> [T]he ideas of economists and political philosophers, both when they are right and when they are wrong, are more powerful than is commonly understood. Indeed, the world is ruled by little else. Practical men, who believe themselves to be quite exempt from any intellectual influences, are usually the slaves of some defunct economist. Madmen in authority, who hear voices in the air, are distilling their frenzy from some academic scribbler of a few years back. I am sure that the power of vested interests is vastly exaggerated compared with the gradual encroachment of ideas.[2]

So the ideas generated by economic theorists have a way—especially if taken up by influential members of the profession—of entering the political agenda. (This is certainly true of the move to privatise government-owned enterprises.) Here we explore four economic rationales for the existence of the firm: economies of scale, risk bearing, asset specificity and monitoring costs.

Why are there so few worker-owned firms? What is the appropriate scale or scope of a firm? Why are conglomerates apparently going the way of the dinosaurs? These questions are a few that economists have been asking in the past twenty years. We provide a brief overview of economists' ideas about the firm, and how our understanding of the theoretical underpinnings of the firm have developed and illuminated the questions above.

A moment's thought will reveal one's mental image of the firm: an owner-manager who hires labour, buys new materials, buys or hires equipment, and coordinates the transformation of these inputs into goods and services which are sold, usually for profit, after all costs have been accounted for, including the opportunity costs of capital. Of course, it may be that the owners have hired managers to make day-to-day decisions, and it may be that such people have their own goals—such as a higher market share—which are not entirely congruent with those of the owners, who may be more interested in short-term profits or the long-term value of their shares. But we ignore here the issues arising from these arrangements and focus on the owner-manager.

Of course, it would be possible to examine the historical evolution of the legal entity of the limited-liability company, for example, but our purpose here is to provide a perspective on possible logical explanations of the firm, and to try to answer the questions posed above.

What have economic theorists had to say about the firm? Ten years before Keynes wrote the words quoted above, Frank Knight[3] had argued that the existence of risk was a possible explanation for the firm.

Knight's firm is one where, because commitments in capital and production processes and inputs must be made before the final demand and price are known, there is risk. He distinguished risk, where the probabilities of certain events can be calculated, from uncertainty, where the likelihoods of events can only be guessed at: risk allows actuarial tools to be used. He argued that the firm allows an efficient allocation of risk between the poorer, perhaps more risk-averse workers and the richer, perhaps less risk-averse owners, who may also have better information with which to direct the firm. The lower risk for the workers is reflected in agreed fixed wages, but the cost of this to the workers is lower returns than if they bore more of the firm's risk. This internal division of labour is both efficient at sharing risk and provides the incentive for owners to monitor labour.

Knight is better known for his rationale for profits, which, he argued, are the reward for forgoing consumption now in order to invest in the firm. Profits also provide the incentive for owners to invest wisely. The owners are the residual risk-bearers who may lose everything but who stand to earn any profits that the firm generates (above the normal competitive return to capital).

The alternative to the coordinating management of the firm is the price-directed mechanism of the market. This raises the question of why the owners of the various inputs (including the knowledge of how to combine them into outputs) could not just come together in the market and reach agreement on the terms of combining their inputs and selling the output, whether good or service. That is, they would write a short-term contract which committed each input owner to a particular level of performance and specified the division of the revenues generated. This is the standard pattern in the theatre, as discussed above.

Writing a few years after Keynes, Ronald Coase[4] argued that writing the contracts necessary for coming together in the market is not costless, and that, as this cost rises, there comes a point at which a less costly alternative is to bring the relationship inside the firm, to substitute managed coordination for price coordination, which obviates the need for a completely specified contract. He called the cost of writing the contract the transaction cost, and noted that unforeseen eventualities (breakdowns, shortages, etc.) would require costly renegotiation of the contracts in the market, or even more costly attempts to anticipate all possible contingencies and specify them in the initial contract. The costs of renegotiation and the price discovery process could be economised by agreement beforehand to a hierarchical authority to sort things out.

More recently, Oliver Williamson[5] has focused not on the cost of Coase's price discovery and negotiation, but on the venture specificity of assets—if a supply relationship is via the market, and the firm's assets rely on input from another firm, then this supplying firm can hold up the buyer: Pay us more, or your firm-specific assets will become worthless! Common ownership of both firms' complementary assets, through vertical integration, will remove this risk and is often seen. An example is General Motors merging with Fisher Body, the independent firm that manufactured its automobile bodies, lest it be held up. An alternative is long-term market relationships, such as seen in the Japanese car industry.

As Armen Alchian and Harold Demsetz[6] argued, there is another cost that may be minimised within the firm: the cost of monitoring work effort. With economies of scale or scope, with joint production and no clear output from the individual worker, and with asymmetric information (workers know more of their abilities and effort than does management), there exist incentives to loaf or free-ride on others' labours. The owner-manager could appoint monitors to deter such behaviour; but this just raises the issue of monitoring the appointed monitors: *Quis custodiet ipsos custodies?* The best-motivated monitor is the person who is the residual claimant—the owner—who has the incentive to monitor most cost effectively in the firm's environment of coordinated management. If there is loafing on the job, then the owner will bear the eventual cost, in terms of lower returns, so the firm provides a means of centralising the monitoring.

Recent cases of certain partners in law firms misappropriating clients' money, and thus imposing a financial burden on the remaining partners, has highlighted the mismatch between risk bearing and monitoring of one's partners' behaviour in such firms. One solution is incorporation, a legal process which minimises the potential losses faced by the new owners—the erstwhile partners—but which does little to reduce the costs of monitoring, absent a clearer hierarchy. The firm, however, includes a hierarchical organisational structure, which thus reduces cost of monitoring and the risk of cheating that the partnership exhibits.

Oliver Hart[7] describes what he calls the property-rights approach, which is best understood by asking what changes hands when one firm acquires another: the answer is the physical or non-human assets of the acquired firm. This ownership, he argues, is a source of power when contracts are incomplete, as they will inevitably be. As well as bearing the residual risk (and reaping any above-normal returns), the owner of an asset has the residual control rights over that asset. A separate supplying firm's management can threaten to make both its own assets and its labour unavailable for any uncontracted-for increase in production. If the increased production is important to the downstream firm, then this may be a costly threat. If the upstream firm were a division of the downstream firm, then the assets would not be under ultimate control of the upstream management. There is thus an incentive for ownership of the supply by the downstream firm, as mentioned in the case of Fisher Body above. This is an extension of Williamson's arguments.

There are sociologists who argue against the self-centred assumptions of the economics models and explanations, but they have not developed a theory of the firm based on altruistic motivations yet. When they do, perhaps Henri Szeps can dramatise it. For all the diversity of explanations of the firm, the assumption of self-centred owners, workers, suppliers and managers is agreed on.

Can we explain why Henri Szeps is not employed in a repertory company, and why in the theatre such arrangements, as we have been motivating with the above discussion, are very unusual? First, the possibilities for economies of scale are small: for centuries theatres' seating capacities have not grown significantly, although machinery has appeared backstage for lighting and sound, as well as for scene changing. So the size of production has not grown, and the number of players has remainded much the same over time. (Given rising standards of living and labour-saving technical progress in other sectors, this poses a challenge for future theatrical productions, which may be priced out of reach of many playgoers; hence Henri's one-man show, and hence the importance of television, where the potential audiences can justify higher wages and costs of actors and others. Television programs, however, are produced by firms.) Second, actors are usually not in a financial position to act as producers, with up-front expenditures and with the possibility of sizeable losses if the production is not popular. Third, with the number of people—actors and backstage—a manageable size, monitoring, especially of the actors, of course, has been relatively inexpensive. (This is even more true of orchestras.) Fourth, there is little possibility of hold-up occurring, although some prima donas might like to think they are indispensible to a production. Plays, theatrical venues, actors, designers, musicians—all are to a greater or lesser extent substitutable, especially in a world where there are additional psychic rewards beyond the merely monetary.

For most enterprises, however, the four explanations discussed above are plausible, and help us see how economic theory can illuminate the existence of the black box known as the firm and its management.

FOR THE MANAGER

This essay was not written to provide the manager with a tangible take-away. Instead, on the premise that we often miss the wood for the trees, the author's aim is to provide a closer look at the economic rationale for the firm, that pervasive institution that we take for granted. Eventually the practical upshots of the analysis described here will become manifest in the legal foundations of future firms, as well as the improved management of risk-bearing, of monitoring, and of the nexus of contracts that comprise the firm.

FURTHER READING

W. Baumol, 'On the Performing Arts: The Anatomy of their Economic Problem', *American Economic Review*, 55, May 1965, pp. 495–502.
This short paper by Baumol, specifically on the future squeeze between box-office receipts and the theatre's wages bill in the absence of continuing technical change, was the first mention of this syndrome, now known as Baumol's disease. Eminently readable.

R. Coase, *The Firm, the Market, and the Law*, Chicago University Press, Chicago, 1988.

We have mentioned Coase's classic contribution of 1937, *The Nature of the Firm*, which is included in this recent compilation. Coase received the 1991 Nobel prize in economics in part for this work. This volume should be seen as a reference, since it is not written for the practising manager, but for the professional economist.

H. Demsetz, *The Economics of the Business Firm: Seven Critical Commentaries*, Cambridge University Press, Cambridge, 1995.
This volume brings together Demsetz's papers and thinking on the nature of the firm, including the theory about the convenience of monitoring workers' efforts that he developed with Alchian, as we mentioned. Not for the practising manager.

O. Hart, *Firm Contracts and Financial Structure*, Clarendon Press, Oxford, 1995.
Hart's writing is even more technical than is Coase's and Demsetz's. Not for the practising manager.

J. Maynard Keynes, *The General Theory of Employment Interest and Money*, Macmillan for the Royal Economic Society, London, 1973, (1936).
Keynes' classic work on the role of government to stimulate aggregate demand at times of deflation. Also noteworthy for his characterisation of the stock market as a 'beauty contest', but one in which the role for each market participant is to guess which 'beauty' will be the most popular with the other participants, rather than guessing who is the most beautiful. Often cited and even quoted, but seldom read, with reason.

J. McMillan, 'Managing Suppliers: Incentive Systems in Japanese and United States Industry', *California Management Review*, 32, 1990, pp. 38–55.
McMillan's article is an eminently readable comparison of the 'relationship' contracting that occurs between Japanese car makers and their suppliers, contrasted with the arm's-length, market relationships between Western car makers and their suppliers. Interesting discussion of the extent and boundaries of the firm.

L. Putterman and R. Kroszner (eds), *The Economic Nature of the Firm: A Reader*, 2nd edn, Cambridge University Press, Cambridge, 1996.
This is the best place to follow up ideas that the author has raised in this essay. As well as several contributions exploring these themes (including articles on Knight and Williamson), it includes an excellent introduction, which is worth the price of the book alone.

H. Szeps, *All in Good Timing: A Personal Account Of What An Actor Does*, Currency Press, Sydney, 1998.
Henri's book has nothing per se to do with this essay, but is the summation of his acting experience. As you'd expect, eminently readable.

5

Knowledge, tacit understanding and strategy

TIMOTHY M. DEVINNEY

He that studies only men, will get the body of knowledge without the soul; and he that studies only books, the soul without the body. He that to what he sees adds observation, and to what he reads, reflection, is on the right road to knowledge.

—Charles Caleb Colton (1780–1832)

Few managers would question the criticality of the management of a firm's strategy to long run success. Yet, it is interesting how few firms manage the development of strategy effectively. This may appear to be a strange statement since few medium- to large-sized organisations lack planning processes and many, if not most, are blessed with MBA-laden corporate planning or business development functions. However, the existence of these functions (corporate planning) and routines (business planning) has little, if anything, to do with the development of strategy. The problem arises from managers' confusion between the tasks of analysis and planning—which are concerned mainly with monitoring performance and resource allocation—and the desired outcome of strategic thinking.

The problems associated with strategy development are due not to the manager's lack of a desire to develop better strategy but to the academics and consultants who profess to possess special powers and techniques that will turn the barren ore of research into the gold of strategic success. Like the alchemists of old, the modern conjurer's techniques get tried and fail but the suckers keep coming back for more. The ultimate prize is so valued that every formula, no matter how ridiculous, must be tried lest a competitor stumble onto it first. In this environment, firms and managers move, herd-like, from one fad to the next. As firms moved from 'diversification' in the 1960s, to 'management by objectives' in the 1970s, to TQM in the 1980s, to 're-engineering' in the 1990s, managers went from T-group training to 'one-minute managing' and are, today, listening to Mormon philosophy about the 'seven habits' that will save them from their inefficient selves.

Unlike the more disciplined areas of business, such as economics, accounting, finance or operations research—where a readily accepted set of theories, rules and methods dominate—the field of strategic management is something of a United Nations of management disciplines. Most academics hail from a host of disciplines, the most obvious being economics and organisation behaviour but with many others represented—anthropology, sociology, population ecology, finance, marketing, political science and theology, to name only a limited number. Add to this the fact that the field of strategy is where many management consultants get their academic seal of approval by teaching at a business school and you have a potent mixture of ideas and egos that makes for some interesting debate. But does it add to our knowledge? Is the debate scientific or purely religious?

Much of the difficulty in understanding and developing strategy arises from the lack of a single agreed upon paradigm. However, over time academic thinking has begun solidifying along what might be considered a 'rationalist' approach to strategic thinking. Figure 5.1 outlines a heavily edited view of the development of strategic thinking in recent decades. The period of the 1960s and 1970s was

Figure 5.1 Evolution in the development of strategic thinking

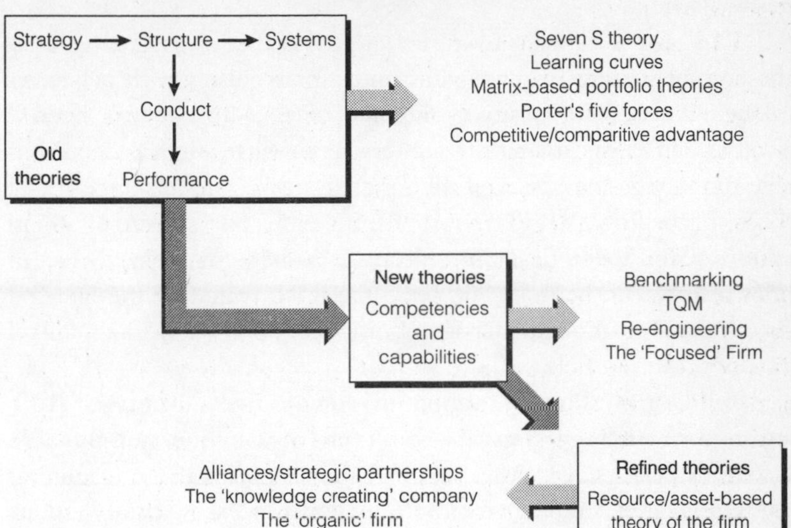

very much a period of pseudo-scientific thinking—learning curves, portfolio matrixes and a raft of organisation behaviour theories dominated. However, in the late 1970s Michael Porter[1] began adding some rigour to management thinking by imbuing it with what one might call 'old-style' industrial organisation theory. The 1980s were a period of consultant-generated pop-philosophy with many ideas being produced and widely accepted by academics and managers without any supporting scientific data. Hamel and Prahalad[2] and Stalk et al.[3] got into a debate reminiscent of the 'how many angels fit on the head of a pin' discussions in the Middle Ages. Hamel and Prahalad defined a notion called competencies while Stalk et al. floated a competing notion they called capabilities (competencies won by the way). Also during this period, and outside the public eye, a great deal of research was being conducted in the fields of information economics and what has been coined the 'new' industrial organisation. From this came a rebirth of ideas associated with early 20th century scholars such as Coase,[4] Hayek,[5] and Schumpeter.[6] The focus of strategy switched from normative techniques to more fundamental questions like: Why do firms exist in the form they do?

Why do we find so many different types of organisations competing in the same market? Why do firms consistently differ in terms of performance?

This change in focus from techniques to thinking has integrated the field of strategic management much more closely with neoclassical economics. The positive outcome of this linkage has been a growing consensus among researchers about what might be a reasonable foundation for a general theory of strategy. The 'resource-based theory of the firm' (RBT) is a rather simple idea but is based on sound empirical and theoretical work rather than the ad hoc empiricism of prior research in the field. Although the RBT is the not the 'general field theory' of strategic management it has found a remarkable level of support in the field.

Building on Porter's notion of competitive advantage, RBT argues that strategy must be built on the unique non-imitable resources possessed by the firm. All firms possess these resources. They appear as brand names, production processes, combinations of human capital assets, patents and technologies, corporate reputation and so on. What makes these resources valuable is not their uniqueness per se but their 'uniqueness in effect'. For example, both Toyota and BMW possess unique resources. However, when it comes to the final production of comparable motor cars, the prices charged and profit made by these companies is quite similar. Toyota's advantage might be in engine design and performance and BMW's in handling and suspension technology. In the end, it is the substitutability of Lexus, BMW and other luxury brands that reduces the impact of the uniqueness of a firm's assets on their profit performance.

Uniqueness in effect will arise either because of *uniqueness*—the firm possesses some unique assets, such as patents—because of its history (*path dependence*), which by definition cannot be duplicated, or because of *causal ambiguity*—no one can quite figure out what the actual combination of assets is that makes the firm special. These latter two situations appear to be the most important. Path dependence is critical since it implies 'history matters'. Hence, firms early into markets can establish advantages that later entrants have no possibility of duplicating. Alternatively, firms may find history an albatross around their necks. IBM had to go on serving old mainframe customers long after it became apparent that the new markets were in smaller machines. Causal ambiguity is double-sided since it implies that we don't actually know what makes us unique. The same confusion that allows a firm to sustain an advantage will also make it difficult to extend that advantage since the firm itself, by definition, cannot understand why it is unique!

Much of the literature that built on Porter's work concentrated on the sustaining of competitive advantage. Unfortunately, sustaining implies that you possessed an advantage in the first place. Recent thinking has begun to deal with this problem by focusing more heavily on the dynamic nature of advantage. This is particularly important since advantages exist only within a specific environmental context. For example, the Coca-Cola brand name is a valuable resource built up over decades of advertising, sales and image management. Unfortunately, the advantage is a disadvantage when it comes to speed of entry. Because the brand name is so valuable, Coca-Cola will only apply it to what it considers to be sure-bet new products. The company will, therefore, be more risk averse than competitors with less valuable intangible assets. Therefore, resources that provide flexibility over a host of environmental and market circumstances are to be preferred to those that provide advantage only in rigid conditions. Similarly, resources that are self-renewing or allow the firm to develop new capabilities are particularly prized since they provide both current and future advantage.

Our discussion to this point implies that true sustainable advantage requires firm's to possess resources that are: (1) unique in effect; (2) lacking in substitutes; (3) flexible, or dynamic; and (4) durable—in the sense that they are either long-lived or have the ability to be self-renewing. Looking at the resources available to the firm, there are few resources that would pass muster on these criteria. Certainly, most tangible resources, such as land, labour costs, raw material inputs and so on, fail as strategic resources. In searching for advantage firms ultimately must rely on the intangible and embedded resources, many of which cannot even be articulated even though they are recognised to exist. Of all these intangible resources, organisational and individual knowledge is the most valuable but also the most difficult to articulate, understand, develop and transfer. It is to this that we now turn.

KNOWLEDGE AS THE ULTIMATE SOURCE OF ADVANTAGE

What is knowledge?

The importance of knowledge to strategic advantage has been recognised for as long as strategy has been developed. However, modern strategic management with its penchant for techniques had, until recently, ignored what was often thought of as a philosophical debate more appropriately left to academics. But as the service component of production increased and as service industries have come to dominate developed economies, the importance of knowledge as an organisationally managed asset made it a topic of ever growing discussion. If the 20th century was the era of industry where victory went to the general with the biggest industrial battalions, the 21st century will surely be the era of services where triumph goes to the general who engages in 'the wise use of . . . knowledge'.[7]

There is a great deal of confusion between knowledge and information as it is commonly used. Figure 5.2 attempts to deal with this as simply as possible. Dretske makes the distinction between information and knowledge quite succinct:

> Information is a commodity capable of yielding knowledge and what information a signal carries is what we can learn from it. Knowledge is information-produced belief.[8]

Information is two-dimensional. It possesses a semantic, or meaning, component that can only be interpreted in light of knowledge and a syntactic, or volume, component. Knowledge is context-specific. It can exist independent of existing information or be enhanced or affected by new information. Action is based, not on information, but on knowledge. Knowledge leads to the formation of beliefs and commitment (to principles and individuals), gives meaning to animate and inanimate things, and serves as the basis of all action. According to classical epistemology, knowl-

Figure 5.2 The relationship between information and knowledge

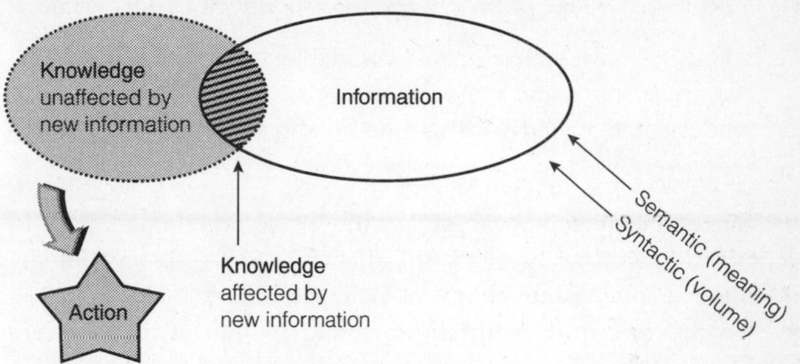

edge is 'justified true belief'—meaning that: (1) knowledge is 'true'; (2) I believe knowledge is 'true' and (3) I am justified in my belief that knowledge is 'true'.

Machlup[9] discusses three types of knowledge: knowing that, knowing what, and knowing how. The most critical of the three definitions is 'knowing how'. 'Knowing that' is what philosophers call *propositional* knowledge, of which classical epistemology's definition is an example—knowing that something is so and not otherwise. For example, we all know that 12 × 12 = 144. 'Knowing what' is an expansion of 'knowing that'. For example, I speak German and know what the German language is. However, I do not know all the nuances of the language and the entire vocabulary. 'Knowing how' is the most critical type of knowledge since it captures William James'[10] idea of 'knowledge about' things as opposed to 'knowledge of' something. Knowing how requires 'systemic study and reflection', judgment, proposition, testing and integration with other forms of know-how.

The importance of know-how

'Knowing how', or know-how, can be the ultimate source of strategic advantage when appropriately embedded within the organisational systems of the firm. As Teece[11] points out, simply knowing how to do something is not a de facto advantage—numerous ways of doing the same thing exist. For example, Nissan's plants in Japan, Mexico and the US use different mixes of technology and labour to create similar cars with approximately similar overall productivity. The competitive advantage of know-how arises under two circumstances:

1 when it is embedded in non-codifiable understanding of customers, systems and markets; and
2 when it is matched with unique combinations of complementary assets.

Since know-how is context specific, those other assets used in combination with knowledge will affect the value and use of the information coming into the firm. Complementary assets are those assets necessary for converting the core know-how of the firm into products and services. These assets have both a generic and a specialised character. Completely generic complementary assets are those that can be bought and sold on the open market. For example, secretarial services are a necessary component of business but there is an open market for secretaries—no one firm's secretaries are necessarily better or worse than any other firm's. Specialised complementary assets are those assets developed specifically for use in combination with the firm's intangible know-how. They are also likely to be co-dependent; that is, they are valuable only in the context in which they are used. Chaparral Steel is a small US steel producer using arch-furnace technology.[12] It does all its research and development on the plant floor—there is no R&D department of which to speak. Chaparral's method of research and product development is unique to the firm. It arose from the necessity of operating a small mini-mill and Chaparral's approach to employee training. Although interesting to study, no other steel mill followed the Chaparral model because it was a method suitable for that firm alone. The reality is that complementary assets will possess a mixture of generic and specialised characteristics.

The strategic question is, of course, what is it about any specific combination of know-how and complementary assets that allows the firm to develop a true sustainable advantage. The firm's strategic assets are more likely to be unique, durable, flexible and less subject to competitors' substitutes, when the relationship between know-how and complementary assets is embedded within the firm. However, the embeddedness of know-how—that which makes it strategic—creates its own problems. For a company to fully capitalise the advantages of know-how it must be able to create and transfer it. However, the sheer act of transferring know-how will, by definition, take away much of its strategic advantage!

The transferring and creation of know-how

Organisations grow by transferring what they know how to do to others. The problem is that the act of transference requires that knowledge be systematised and codified. The object of growth and expansion requires that the tacit understanding of how to do something must be made explicit so that it can be communicated to others. To the extent that know-how can be codified, its durability declines and the likelihood of acceptable substitutes increases. For example, many pharmaceutical firms suffer from the fact that the know-how of scientific teams becomes codifiable as soon as the relevant compound or method is developed. This forces firms to use other techniques to protect their investment. One approach is to patent the discovery—an imperfect solution in many cases. For example, American Home Product Corporation operated as a 'rapid follower' in the pharmaceutical industry. It produced products 'similar' to those patented by other companies, thereby avoiding the costs of creating knowledge incurred by its competitors. A second approach is to bundle drug discovery with complementary assets in marketing and distribution. This ensures that know-how is protected to the extent that the firm is able to convert it into more products for more people.

Some know-how is only imperfectly codifiable and requires an enormous personal investment in specific understanding. A classic example of weak codifiability is brewing technology. Breweries live and die by the ability to train brewmasters and it is generally the lack of brewmasters that limits expansion. Brewing beer is mainly science but becoming a fully fledged brewmaster can take twenty years of on-the-job training. Know-how comes mainly from doing.

Figure 5.3 represents the cycle that is necessary for the transference of know-how. Nonaka and Takeuchi[13] have extensively studied this process. The goal is to create new tacit understanding

Figure 5.3 The know-how transfer cycle

Receiver

Tacit knowledge ⟶ Explicit knowledge

Source: Tacit knowledge ⟵ Explicit knowledge

Tacit knowledge	Socialisation Sympathised knowledge	Externalisation Conceptual knowledge
Explicit knowledge	Internalisation Operational knowledge	Combination Systemic knowledge

Ω Δ Φ Γ

Source: I. Nonaka and H. Takeuchi, *The Knowledge Creating Company*, Oxford University Press, New York, 1995.

from old tacit know-how. To get to this point, a firm must be able to convert its implicit understanding into codified *conceptual knowledge*. This must then be combined with the existing knowledge base of the individual. At this point the knowledge is *systemic*—actually it has ceased to be knowledge and is really information. This knowledge must then be internalised by the receiver into their *operational knowledge* of how to do something. Finally, the individual must be able to meld the know-how into their internal schemas through *socialisation*.

At each stage in this process there will be errors. These errors may be misinterpretations, communication gaps, a failure to transfer ideas completely, and so on. If we denote these possible errors by the Greek symbols on the figure, we see that in just one attempt to transfer our know-how we have missed by $\Omega + \Delta + \Phi + \Gamma$. Recognising that this process is ongoing, it becomes clear that after a few iterations, the knowledge base of the organisation can look nothing like what it did originally. This will be most likely in those circumstances where knowledge is least codifiable and the firm is attempting to transfer what may be essentially impossible to transfer.

This points out the double-edged nature of know-how. Take the case of Chaparral Steel once again. At one point in the early 1990s, they considered expanding operations by building another plant at a new greenfield location. However, the uniqueness of its know-how and the inability to duplicate it except through long, hard socialisation led to their decision to expand slowly at their existing location. Whether or not this was the right decision is difficult to say, but it does show sensitivity on the part of the company to the limitations its unique know-how imposes on it.

The management of a firm's knowledge system is composed of: (1) the creation of know-how; (2) the management of the codification of that system; and (3) the management of the transfer of that knowledge. It also points out the importance of know-how as an integral part of the company's strategic thinking.

Time has three effects on knowledge. First knowledge can become obsolete. As with any asset, management must ensure that reinvestment occurs so that the quality of the asset is maintained. The most obvious mechanisms are internally created knowledge (for example, through R&D, training, and daily learning and experimentation) or through the acquisition of external knowledge (for example, through the hiring of new employees, linkages to or acquisitions of other firms, external training, consultants or intellectual 'borrowing' from competitors). Second, firms can forget know-how. Forgetting arises from obsolescence but is most likely to occur from cost-cutting, downsizing and outsourcing, including shifting production overseas. Third, as knowledge ages it tends to become codified and standardised. This is inevitable, as expansion demands the codification and transference of know-how. Systems and strategies must be in place to protect the strategic advantage received from know-how as it becomes more and more a commodity.

In reality, all firms gather mounds of information and create know-how. The problem is they don't know what to do with it and don't manage it in a self-renewing way. Many firms, learning little from the failure of corporate planning departments, have gone so far as to create 'Chief Knowledge Officers' (CKOs) in the hope that knowledge can be managed if someone is given that responsibility. Such actions are potentially self destructive since management requires measurement and measurement requires codification. The CKO's job should not only be the managing of the stock of know-how but also the responsibility for the management of the three points given above. Only in this way can a firm ensure that the maximum profitability possible is extracted from its knowledge and tacit understanding. Too tight a management of the knowledge system can reduce the flexibility to create new know-how and thereby serve to do little more than perpetuate erroneous knowledge and beliefs.

CONCLUSION: KNOWLEDGE AS SOCIO-COGNITIVE ADVANTAGE

The goal of the management of knowledge is the creation of socio-cognitive advantage. We can think of socio-cognitive advantage as operational advantages that arise from the knowledge management system. It is the output of the tacit and explicit understanding of the firm.

According to Ginsberg,[14] socio-cognitive advantage arises from the complex interaction of the human capital resources of the firm, the organisational resources, and the complex ongoing choices made in the management of strategy. An adaption of Ginsberg's idea is shown in Figure 5.4. It is not important to understand the entire figure but to note that this complex interaction leads to three things (three Cs)—creativity, comprehensiveness and consensus. Creativity is the extent to which a company is able to be innovative in its ability to solve problems—what we would normally think of as product, service or process innovation. Comprehensiveness reflects the degree to which the organisation gathers and retrieves information and synthesises it into knowledge that is an effective contribution to problem solving. Finally, consensus is decision-making know-how—the extent to which the firm's method of making choices is knowledge-based. The point of this discussion is the criticality of all three Cs. A firm can be comprehensive and creative, however, if the power structures within the organisation are such that decision-making is itself not a knowledge based process, all that creativity and comprehensiveness is wasted money and effort.

Figure 5.4 Knowledge as socio-cognitive advantage

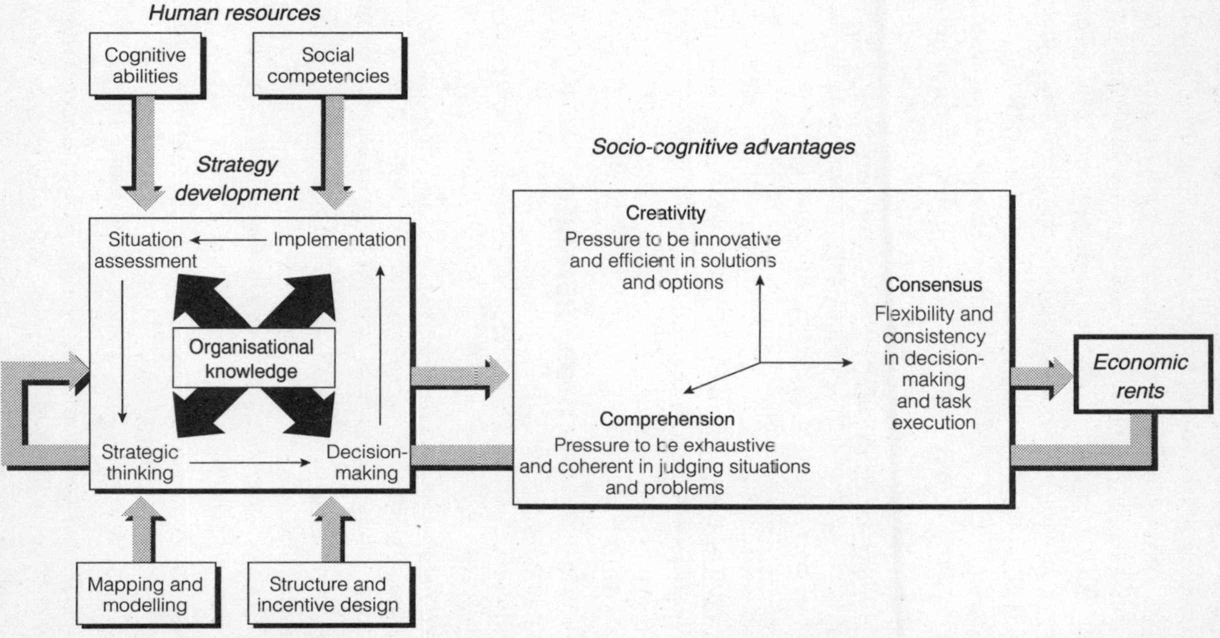

Source: *Adapted from Ginsberg*

It almost goes without saying that knowledge alone does not determine a corporation's strategy or success in total but is a key determinant of performance at the margin. An army does not win victories solely based on the knowledge of its generals, colonels, lieutenants and sergeants but on the relative level of its training, matériel and motivation. However, no opponent can go onto the field of battle without assuming that its opponent has equal access to its complement of training, matériel and motivation. Like many other resources in which a firm invests, knowledge is misused and subject to erosion over time. However, unlike these other assets, knowledge has the capability, if managed well, to be self-renewing and to improve with use. However, the management of that which is rarely seen, little understood and slow to arise is difficult, if not impossible, in a world of quarterly budgets. Perhaps we can only learn from the words of the Hitopadesa:

> Let this be an example for the acquisition of knowledge . . . by the fall of drops of water, by degrees, a pot is filled.[15]

FURTHER READING

Books

M. Boisot, *Knowledge Assets: Securing Competitive Advantage in the Information Economy*, Oxford University Press, Oxford, 1998.
An interesting work by one of Europe's leading organisation theorists.

J. Dancy, *An Introduction to Contemporary Epistemology*, Basil Blackwell, Oxford, 1985.
A primer on the philosophy of knowledge for those wanting the 'brainy' background.

F. Dretske, *Knowledge and the Flow of Information*, MIT Press, Cambridge MA, 1981.
An absolute classic but not for the faint of heart.

P. Drucker, *The Post Capitalist Society*, Butterworth-Heinemann, Oxford, 1993.
One of Drucker's classics.

D. Leonard-Barton, *Well-Springs of Knowledge: Building and Sustaining the Sources of Innovation*, Harvard Business School Press, Cambridge MA, 1995.
A nice introduction to knowledge and innovation for the manager.

P. Moser, and A. Nat, *Human Knowledge*, Oxford University Press, Oxford, 1987.
An excellent book on the psychology of knowledge.

A. Musgrave, *Common Sense, Science and Scepticism*, Cambridge University Press, Cambridge, 1993, Chapters 1, 2, 14 and 15.
A simple and pleasant introduction to the philosophy of knowledge.

R. Nelson, and S. Winter, *An Evolutionary Theory of Economic Change*, Harvard University Press, Cambridge MA, 1982.
A classic on the evolution of change from two leading economists.

R. Pearce, *Global Competition and Technology: Essays in the Creation and Application of Knowledge by Multinationals*, St Martins Press, London, 1997.
A fine introduction to knowledge advantages possessed by multinational enterprises.

M. Polyani, *The Tacit Dimension*, Routledge & Kegan Paul, London, 1966.
The modern classic in the philosophy of knowledge.

M. Ryan, *Knowledge Diplomacy: Global Competition and the Politics of Intellectual Property*, Brookings Institution, Washington, 1998.
A very good, recently published treatise on intellectual property and politics.

Articles

P. Almeida, 'Knowledge Sourcing by Foreign Multinationals: Patent Citation Analysis in the US Semiconductor Industry', *Strategic Management Journal*, 17, 1996, pp. 155–65.
A technical piece on measuring knowledge sourcing. Tough but insightful.

Anonymous, 'Best Practice and Beyond', *McKinsey Quarterly*, 1, 1998, pp. 19–25.
A good introduction for managers about best practice in knowledge management.

M. Appleyard, 'How Does Knowledge Flow? Interfirm Patterns in the Semiconductor Industry', *Strategic Management Journal*, 17, 1996, pp. 137–54.
Presents the results of a survey of knowledge gathering in the semiconductor design sector.

P. Bierly, and A. Chakrabarti, 'Generic Knowledge Strategies in the US Pharmaceutical Industry', *Strategic Management Journal*, 17, 1996, pp. 123–35.
An application to pharmaceuticals.

T. Davenport and L. Prusak, 'Successful Knowledge Management Projects', *Sloan Management Review*, 39, 2, 1998, pp. 43–57.
Davenport is a 'knowledge guru' and this is a fairly good overview of the thinking of one of the managerial visionaries.

S. Davis and J. Botkin, 'Coming of Knowledge-based Business', *Harvard Business Review*, 75, 5, 1994, 165–70.
A nice businessperson's introduction to where people thought we were going a few years back.

F. Hayek, 'The Use of Knowledge in Society', *American Economic Review*, 35, 4, 1945, pp. 519–30.
An absolute classic.

G. Hedlund, 'A Model of Knowledge Management and the N-Form Corporation', *Strategic Management Journal*, 15, (special issue), 1994, pp. 73–90.
A very good introduction to knowledge and organisation structure by one of the leading European academics who passed on in his prime.

A. Inkpen and P. Beamish, 'Knowledge, Bargaining Power and the Instability of International Joint Ventures', *Academy of Management Review*, 22, 1, 1997, pp. 177–202.
This and the next article are part of a larger project started by the University of Western Ontario.

A. Inkpen and D. Dinur, 'Knowledge Management Processes and International Joint Venture', *Organization Science*, 9, 4, 1998, pp. 454–68.

B. Kogut and U. Zander, 'Knowledge of the Firm and the Evolutionary Theory of the Multinational Corporation', *Journal of International Business Studies*, 24, 4, 1993, pp. 625–45 plus the follow-ups of this article by: J. Love (pp. 399–407), D. McFetridge (pp. 409–15), and B. Kogut and U. Zander (pp. 417–26), *Journal of International Business Studies*, 26, 2, 1995.
These articles were the first academic articles to start the ball rolling on knowledge and multinational firm success.

B. Levitt and J. March, 'Organizational Learning', *Annual Review of Sociology*, 14, 1998, pp. 319–40.
A very readable classic on how organisations learn.

'Mini Case: Sharing Knowledge Through BP's Virtual Team Network', *Harvard Business Review*, 75, 5, 1997 pp. 152–3.

I. Nonaka, 'A Dynamic Theory of Organizational Knowledge Creation', *Organization Science*, 5, 1, 1994, pp. 14–37.
A good analog to the Nonaka and Takeuchi book.

P. Strawson, 'Truth', *Analysis*, 9, 6, 1949, pp. 83–97.
A fine little philosophical treatise.

G. Szulanski, 'Exploring Internal Stickiness: Impediments to the Transfer of Best Practice within the Firm', *Strategic Management Journal*, 17, 1996, pp. 27–43.
A good introduction to internal knowledge transfer.

D. Teece, 'Capturing Value from Knowledge Assets', *California Management Review*, 40, 3, 1988, pp. 55–79.
The introductory article to a special issue of the CMR on knowledge. Look at the whole issue if you get a chance.

6

Corporate super-brands: the roles of corporate image and reputation

GRAHAME DOWLING

The purest treasure mortal times afford
is spotless reputation, that away,
men are but gilded loam or painted clay.

—William Shakespeare, *Richard II*

While Shakespeare and other social commentators have long known the importance of personal reputations, most business enterprises only realised the value of a reputation when they started to use branding to identify their company and its products in the late 1800s. Since then, the use of product and corporate brands has become ubiquitous. Over the last twenty years economists, marketers and consultants have been interested in measuring and evaluating corporate brands, and their components—corporate identity, image and reputation. While each group tends to use (and abuse) the terms in a different way, they have all focused on the role of corporate images and reputations in adding value to the firm. This work has led to the images and reputations of a company being designated as one of its major strategic assets.

Economists examined how a firm's reputation can signal its quality to customers and its future intentions to competitors.[1] In this way, the reputation a customer or manager holds of the organisation sets their expectations about the behaviour of that firm. Marketers focused on the construct of corporate image. This is defined as the perceptions and evaluation of a firm and its positioning relative to its competitors.[2] The firm's image can provide marketing support to its products and services by signalling reliability and trustworthiness. This then helps reduce the perceived risk of dealing with the firm. There are many large consulting firms working in this area. Traditionally, their focus has been on how a firm's corporate identity symbols can influence its corporate image.[3] Corporate identity symbols are thought to act as a touchstone for the firm's communications with employees and customers—thus playing a key role in the formation of corporate images.

The scientific and consulting research done over the last two decades indicates that the images and reputations people hold of a company are one of its most important strategic assets. The recently advanced resource-based theory of how firms develop a sustainable competitive advantage suggests that it is this type of intangible and inimitable asset that can help to achieve above average returns on the firm's investments.[4] For example, research by Peter Roberts and myself which examines the financial performance of *Fortune 500* companies in the US suggests that firms with an above average image and reputation in their industry demonstrate the ability to achieve and sustain an above average return on their assets.[5] Various other studies have found a relationship between corporate images and reputations and financial performance.[6]

Research studies and anecdotal evidence suggest that good images and reputations effect performance in the following ways:

- add extra psychological value to products (for example, trust) and service (for example, when it is difficult to evaluate the quality of a service, then it will be rated slightly higher from a company with a good as opposed to a poor reputation);
- increase employee job satisfaction (good companies seem to exert a halo effect on employee job satisfaction ratings);
- provide access to better quality employees when recruiting (most people would rather work for a highly respected company);

- increase advertising and sales-force effectiveness (by boosting the credibility of these corporate communications);
- support new product introductions (for example, the launch of Windows 95 from Microsoft was delayed several times—but customers waited for it);
- act as a powerful signal to competitors (for example, Procter & Gamble once had a reputation for its quick and savage reaction to a competitor's price cut);
- provide access to the best professional service providers (for example, the best advertising agencies want to work for the best clients—so they can 'rent' their reputations);
- provide a second chance in the event of a crisis (for example, Johnson & Johnson suffered two product tampering attacks on its Tylenol brand of analgesic—its market share bounced back each time);
- help raise capital on the equity market (for example, the year before Qantas became a public company it made an after-tax profit of $156 million on revenues of $6.6 billion—not enough to buy one new jumbo jet! Yet, the float was fully subscribed).

Alternatively, poor images and reputations can be dangerous to a company's health:

- many CEOs say that if the share market doesn't like their company it will undervalue its share price;
- journalists seem to pay particular attention to poorly reputed companies, and even when they do something good, they remind their audience that this company has a bad history;
- customers seem more concerned and price sensitive about products and services from less well respected companies;
- poor (external) reputations tend to 'feed' poor employee morale (for example, in 1996 Air India's poor domestic reputation fed considerable employee discontent).

Each year *Fortune* magazine publishes a ranking of 'America's Most Admired Companies'. In 1998 the Top 10 performers, as rated by managers and company analysts, were:

1 General Electric
2 Microsoft

3 Coca-Cola
4 Intel
5 Hewlett-Packard
6 Southwest Airlines
7 Berkshire Hathaway
8 Disney
9 Johnson & Johnson
10 Merck.[7]

There are few surprises here. It is easy to think of a number of reasons why each company would be a corporate super-brand.

What is intriguing about corporate images and reputations however, is that some companies seem to have a far better image and reputation than their marketplace performance suggests they should. Consider the Qantas example mentioned above. Why would an airline that struggles to make a profit from a huge turnover in a highly competitive and unprofitable industry command so much widespread respect? What is the key to their corporate super-brand status? Two other such high-profile examples are the cosmetics retailer, the Body Shop, and Richard Branson's Virgin group of companies. Both are small players in very competitive industries with questionable management competency.

One of the keys to understanding what makes the Top 10 of America's Most Admired Companies corporate super-brands *and* companies like the Body Shop, Qantas and Virgin attain a status above their measured performance, is to understand the difference between the image of a company and its reputation. With this as our foundation, it becomes clear that there are two routes to super-brand status. One is to offer good functional value to stakeholders. The other is to offer good psychological value to stakeholders. In essence, you can perform well, or if you can't be a top performer, be emotional. If a company can both perform well and tap into the emotions of its key stakeholders, it can become an icon-brand like The Walt Disney Company.

After discussing the components of corporate super-brands, this chapter turns its attention to managing the development of corporate images and reputations, and traps to avoid when setting out to enhance these drivers of corporate super-brands.

CORPORATE IDENTITY, IMAGE AND REPUTATION

Many managers, consultants and academics use the terms identity, image and reputation interchangeably. Bundling the three concepts together hides the path to creating a better corporate image and reputation. The most common example of this occurs when a company changes its corporate identity symbols in the hope that this alone will improve its standing in the marketplace. By treating each factor as a different construct, it becomes possible to build a framework to guide change. The following definitions provide the foundations for this framework.[8]

Corporate identity: the visual symbols and nomenclature an organisation uses to identify itself to people (such as the corporate name, logo, typeface, colours, livery, and advertising slogan).

Corporate image: the global evaluation (comprised of a set of beliefs and feelings) a person has about an organisation.

Corporate reputation: the attributed values (such as credibility, honesty, responsibility and integrity) evoked from the person's corporate image.

Figure 6.1 shows how these constructs are related to each other.

The definitions and Figure 6.1 suggest a number of things. First, corporate reputation is a deeper construct than corporate image. The reason for this is that the attributes that describe a company's performance are only really intermediate effects. What makes a super-brand company is when these attributes lead to the organisation being perceived as authentic, credible, honest, reliable and so forth. That is, when the corporate image fits what people think are the appropriate roles and behaviour for the company, it evokes a new set of beliefs about the organisation. This is the organisation's corporate reputation. If this reputation is good, then the organisation is held in esteem and respect; people will have trust and confidence in its actions, and be prepared to support it.

The second insight from Figure 6.1 is that mangers can only hope to change the desired image of their organisation and watch how these beliefs and feelings link to peoples' values and thus create a better reputation. The values held by people, and what they consider to be appropriate roles and behaviour for an organisa-

Figure 6.1 Corporate identity, image and reputation

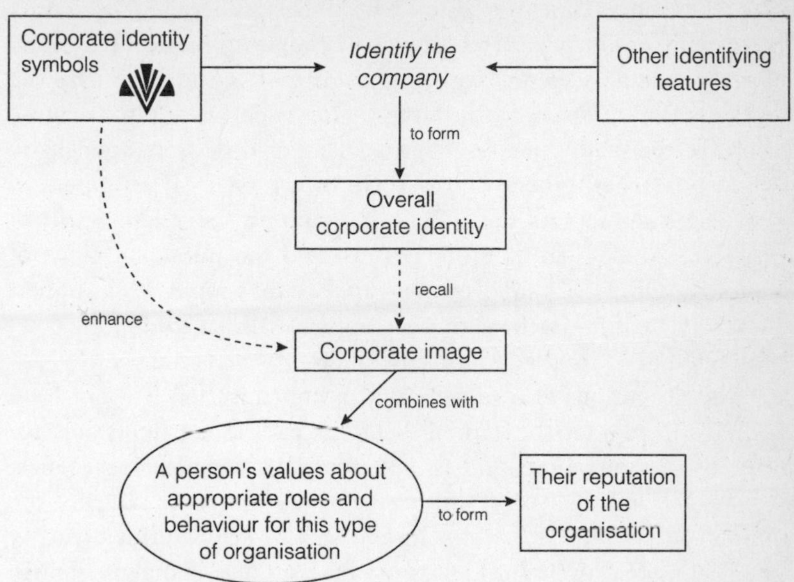

tion will be formed over their lifetime and be very difficult for a single organisation to change. Hence, the task of the manager is to isolate how the attributes of the corporate image tap into peoples' values to create the attributes of the corporate reputation, and then how these lead to confidence, trust and support. Research is the key to uncovering these relationships.

A good corporate reputation will flow naturally from a company that gets high ratings on the types of variables measured in the *Fortune* 'Most Admired Companies' index, namely: innovativeness, quality of management, employee talent, quality of products and services, long-term investment value, financial soundness, social responsibility, and use of corporate assets. *Fortune* argues that top financial performance is a necessary, but not sufficient, condition for a company to rate well in its survey.[9]

A second strategy is for an organisation to understand the freestanding values of its key stakeholders and position its products and services, its behaviour (for example, employment practices and sponsorships) and its communication to fit these values. Two common vehicles for this image positioning are public relations and corporate and/or brand advertising.[10] This is the strategy that has made companies like the Body Shop, Disney, Harley-Davidson, Qantas and Virgin respected beyond their performance. The Body Shop appeals to a counter-culture group that is turned off by the excesses of the cosmetics industry. The Walt Disney Company's vision is to 'make people happy'. Harley-Davidson appeals to (would be) 'rebel' bikers who want to own a piece of an American legend. Qantas targets travellers who want to feel 'The Spirit of Australia'. The Virgin group of brands, and the publicity stunts of its quirky CEO Richard Branson, appeal to people who support challenger brands. Each of these companies links itself to a powerful value held by a group of customers.

The definitions also suggest that an organisation will not have an image or reputation. Rather, different people are likely to have different sets of beliefs and values about an organisation. Hence, they will all hold (slightly) different images and reputations of the same organisation. The most common way to manage this diversity is to assume that different groups of organisational stakeholders will hold different images and reputations. Figure 6.2 identifies the most common groups.

Figure 6.2 Stakeholder groups

A common question is 'Which groups are the most important?'. Employees and customers are always important. After this, it depends on what the organisation does. In most cases, there will be four or five groups to monitor. The challenge is to understand which beliefs and feelings (that is, image) and attributed values (that is, reputation) are similar and different across the various stakeholder groups. Research is the only reliable way to develop this understanding.

CREATING BETTER CORPORATE IMAGES AND REPUTATIONS

A strong set of desired images and reputations for an organisation among stakeholder groups is typically built on four foundations. Each requires some self-analysis and often some changes to be made. Hence, creating better corporate images and reputations can be time consuming and expensive.

What do we want to stand for?

The answer to this question is like a three-legged stool. One leg involves the analysis of what is offered to customers. The key issue here is to communicate what it is that is *important*, *deliverable* and *unique* about your offer. For example, the SWATCH watch company is all about providing a product which can be described as 'fashion that ticks'; the NSW Department of School Education is in the business of providing 'education for life' (life skills and for the rest of your life); Apple Computer focuses on making personal computers which provide the opportunity for people to enhance their skills. For many years this was expressed in their famous corporate slogan 'the power to be your best'. BMW used its engineering expertise to produce cars it labelled in its advertising as 'the ultimate driving machine' and motor bikes as 'the ultimate riding machine'.

Being able to clearly and succinctly articulate the essence of your offer to customers is important. It is equally important however, to stipulate exactly what it is that you offer to your employees—the second leg of the stool. Employees, like customers, listen mostly to the FM radio station with the call sign of WII-FM—'what's in it for me'. An organisation's formal policies (for example, performance-appraisal scheme, pay levels, work practices and so on), organisational culture (for example, informal practices, fun and rituals and so forth), and expectations (for example, rewards for past behaviour, vision statement and so forth) all combine to create an offer to employees.

A senior manager of Citibank in the US once commented that 'how you treat your employees sets the upper limit on how they will treat their customers'. While there are some exceptions to this insight, it seems to capture the essence of the corporate image problem facing many organisations. The image of unhappy (and striking) employees soon gets picked up by external stakeholders and reflected in their images of the organisation.

The third leg of the stool involves the organisation's ethical contribution. Daniel Gross, the editor of the US business magazine *Forbes*, says that 'the ethical heart of business is service to others'.[11] A good example of this is the Wal-Mart discount department store chain. Sam Walton, the founder of Wal-Mart, gave rural Americans, people of modest means, more choice and quality for less cost than ever before. Did customers want this—*yes*. Were employees proud to provide this service—*yes*. Did the community value it—*yes*. Could competitors easily match it—*no*.

Generally the companies with the best images and reputations offer the best value (benefits minus the cost) to their internal and external stakeholders—it's that simple! Research from the Strategic Planning Institute's PIMS (Profit Impact of Market Strategy) data base (empirical analysis of financial and operational data on 3000 businesses) suggests how companies implement this strategy. The PIMS data indicate that perceived product quality is the single most important contributor to return on investment among the wide range of variables measured.[12]

What drives our corporate images?

There are two broad sets of factors that combine to form the desired image an organisation wishes to project. However, only one set of these is under the direct control of managers and can be considered as levers to pull when engineering change. The other set of factors act as a constraint or an opportunity on what can be achieved. The controllable factors are:

- vision;
- organisational culture;
- formal policies (which includes strategy);
- employees;
- products and services;
- advertising and promotion;
- corporate identity; and
- public relations.

The uncontrollable factors are:

- competitors' actions and images;
- country and industry images; and
- media dispositions towards your industry and organisation.

Figure 6.3 shows how these factors combine to produce the image a company projects to its internal and external stakeholders.

The best way to 'attack' Figure 6.3 is from left to right. Many organisations have a weak foundation from which to project a good corporate image because there is a poor fit between the first three controllable internal factors: vision, organisational culture and formal policies. Human resource people capture the essence of this problem in the saying that 'people do what is inspected, in preference to what is expected'.[13] In other words, if your formal policies (for example, employee performance appraisal) reward, say, cost cutting and your vision statement applauds customer service, employees will always give cost cutting first preference, regardless of how important customer service is to projecting a good image.

An organisation's product/service offering and its promotion are potentially the key drivers of corporate image. Figure 6.3 suggests that it is not only the external stakeholders (particularly customers) who are interested in the value of what is offered, but employees are probably just as interested. In fact, employees are increasingly being labelled as advertising's 'second audience'.[14]

If we focus on customers as a key external group, Figure 6.3 suggests that at least four factors drive the images that they hold

Figure 6.3 Factors that drive corporate images

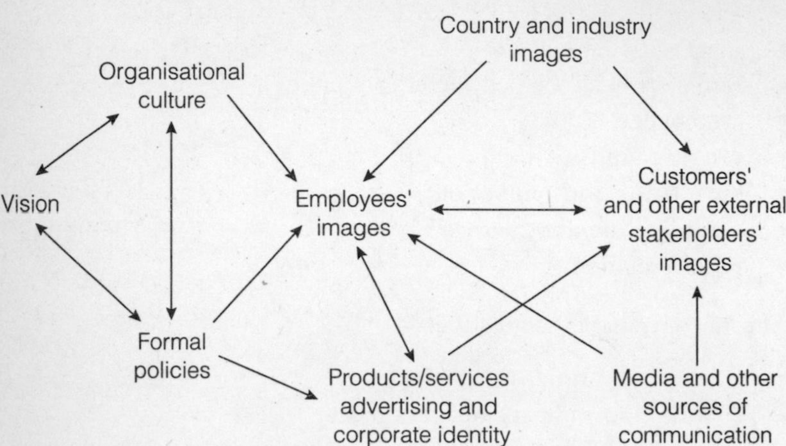

of an organisation, namely: the perceived value of the offering, their perceptions of employees (for example, do they have a customer focus?), what other people and the media are saying about the organisation, and whether or not the organisation is part of a well respected industry (this includes the images of competitors). The discipline of marketing suggests that the most important of these factors is the perceived value of products and services.

While Figure 6.3 provides an overview of the major foundations (vision, culture and formal policies), drivers (employees, the product/service offer, communications) and constraints (the uncontrollable factors) of an organisation's images, it is somewhat misleading! The reason for this was touched on previously, namely, different stakeholders will have different relationships with the organisation. This means that Figure 6.3 needs to be reworked before deciding how to improve the desired image for a particular stakeholder group. Table 6.1 shows some different sets of variables to consider for three groups.

Before setting out to engineer change for a particular group, it is necessary to identify the key variables and then remodel Figure 6.3 so that it reflects the inter-relationships among them. In effect, this becomes the organisation's blueprint for change.

Table 6.1 Key corporate image drivers

Stakeholder group	Key variables	
Employees	• CEO • vision • formal policies • organisational culture	• advertising • products • service • publicity
Customers	• product/service value • advertising • competitors' offers	• publicity • employees • community service
Financial analysts	• past and expected financial performance • CEO, top management team, strategy • industry performance	

Stamp out stupid practices

A quick way to damage both the organisation's image and reputation is to be perceived as either wasteful, greedy, stupid, or when it is perceived that the organisation discriminates among similar types of people, has power over them or doesn't trust them. Nearly every organisation has one or more practices that signal these attributes to their stakeholders. The easiest ones to identify are those which upset customers and employees. Here are some classics.

- Use lawyers to talk to valued customers. For example, the application forms for both Qantas and Ansett Australia's frequent-flyer schemes contain some very heavy-handed terms and conditions. These leave the impression that the airlines don't trust their most valuable customers!
- For the last few Christmas holiday periods, the petrol companies have raised the pump price of a litre of petrol by up to five cents! Also, during any week the pump price can vary by five cents or more per litre. This doesn't instil customer confidence in the petrol company's pricing policies.
- In their search to attract new customers and employees, some companies offer them a better deal than their existing (loyal) employees and customers.

The point about these types of practices is that they cause stakeholders to lose confidence in an organisation. When confidence is eroded, it eats away at key attributes of corporate reputation such as honesty and fairness. The only way to identify practices that destroy the image and reputation of an organisation is to periodically ask each group of important stakeholders.

Communicating with internal and external stakeholders

The final element in creating a better corporate image is communication—to external audiences via advertising and publicity, and to internal audiences via advertising, meetings, internal documents and word-of-mouth. One of the critical elements of a good corporate image is positioning the organisation to stand for something important, deliverable, and *different*. Most organisations fail the unique part of this test. When this happens, customers tend to focus on price. If a company's offer is not significantly different from others, then why shouldn't customers buy the cheapest?

The corporate slogans that companies have and sometimes their name are often used to communicate their positioning. Consider some examples:

- 3M—innovation;
- Qantas—the spirit of Australia;
- Sharp—sharp minds; sharp products; and
- Sydney Water—good enough to bottle; too good to waste.

Some corporate slogans work just as well with employees as customers. For example, the Nike slogan 'just do it' says to customers to stop being a couch potato, buy the product and get out and use it. It also says to employees to be proactive and get things done. In the case of 3M, the single word 'innovation' communicates to every employee the key driver of corporate success.

IMAGE AND REPUTATION TRAPS

There are many traps that catch the unwary manager who sets out to improve his or her organisation's desired corporate image. Six of the more common ones are described below. Each can be costly in terms of wasted time, effort and money. For example, it is not uncommon for the full costs (including managers' time) of a big corporate identity change project like that undertaken by the Commonwealth Bank and Telstra in the early 1990s, to exceed $10 million and take a number of years to complete.

The single image/reputation trap

Probably the most common mistake is to forget that images and reputations are held in the minds of stakeholders, and that different groups will think differently about your organisation. This trap causes some nasty problems. First, there is often confusion and counter-arguing among managers and other employees about whether or not there is an image problem. Second, there is a good chance that change directed at improving the desired image of one group will upset another group of stakeholders. For example, a classic in recent years has been the efforts of senior managers to 're-engineer' their organisations to impress (institutional) shareholders at the expense of employee morale and sometimes customer images.

The corporate identity equals corporate image trap

There are a number of reasons why an organisation should change its corporate identity symbols. Some of these are: to update a tired identity; to signal a change of strategy or operations; to reflect the merging of two companies; because the old name is out of date (Minnesota Mining and Manufacturing to 3M); to get rid of a mean-nothing name; to rent a more powerful name (Amatil to Coca-Cola Amatil). Many corporate identities, however, are changed for less valid reasons, for example: because a new CEO or marketing director doesn't like the old identity; to hide from poor performance; because the advertising agency or a design consultant says it is a good idea.

The identity equals image trap is all about being fully aware of the likely impact of changing your corporate identity symbols. As Figures 6.1 and 6.3 suggest, a cosmetic change to your corporate identity (and nothing else) is highly unlikely to improve either your desired corporate image or your reputation. It may help customers find you, but their images will be formed more by the value of your offer, than the corporate packaging.

Corporate advertising traps

There is a wide-ranging debate among both managers and advertising agencies as to the value of corporate as opposed to brand advertising. The three key issues here are that, if corporate advertising is used, remember to:

1 make it interesting from the target audience member's point of view (as opposed to management's viewpoint);
2 try to incorporate the organisation's core benefit (and/or product benefits) in the theme of the advertising; and
3 make sure it reflects the positioning of the organisation.

Also, remember that employees are advertising's second audience—so make sure that they understand why you are using this type of advertising.

Treat your employees like mushrooms and keep them in the dark

Corporate image change programs are generally sensitive, and sometimes controversial, issues. Hence, they are often planned in secrecy. The positive effect of surprising competitors, however, is often outweighed by the negative effects secrecy has on employees, namely:

1 many will feel that they are not trusted;
2 marketing managers will feel that they should have had a major role in what they perceive is essentially a marketing project; and
3 it is difficult to gain widespread internal support for the change program.

Because employees generally have most to gain and lose from a new desired image, informing them about such change only hours before the media often loses their confidence and support.

Ignoring strong country and industry images

Sometimes, corporate images are bound up with the images which people hold of countries and industries. The trap here is not to appreciate that country and industry images may support or counter the desired image of your company. For example, the use of Paul Hogan and Elle McPherson in tourist advertisements for Australia firmly positions Australia as 'the land of the long-weekend'. We project an image as a friendly and interesting place to holiday. This is a great asset for any company dealing with tourism, leisure or related activities. But it does little to help companies manufacturing for export. The task here is to understand what people currently believe about the country and/or industry they associate with an organisation, and then search through the components of these images for something to build on.[15] It is generally not a good idea to try to argue with stakeholders that their images are wrong. Governments often employ such a strategy when they support 'buy Australian/Canadian/US' advertising campaigns.

Failing to measure

There is an old saying in management that 'if you can't measure it, you can't manage it'. This advice is well taken when setting out to evaluate the super-brand status of an organisation. The key variables to measure for each key stakeholder group are: the familiarity and relevance of the organisation for these stakeholders;[16] their images; freestanding values, reputations, and the levels of confidence, trust and support. Without such a full-profile measure it is difficult to understand (1) the components of the corporate super-brand, (2) the overlap of evaluations across stakeholder groups, and (3) how changes to the factors identified in Figure 6.3 will flow through to affect image, reputation and the vital outcomes of confidence, trust and support. In effect, without a structured approach to measurement, potential changes are made in a fog.

A second aspect of this trap is to report a scorecard (or beauty contest) measure of corporate image to senior managers. Many of these appear each year in the business press and they typically annoy senior managers—especially when a competitor gets a higher rating. These measures are generally composed of five to ten scales that mix up aspects of identity, image and reputation. (They ignore stakeholder freestanding values which may provide the key to creating a good reputation for most organisations.) What gets reported in the business press is an overall (summed) rating and/or ranking for each company that is almost useless for managers wanting to improve their corporate status.

A PROGRAM FOR CHANGING YOUR DESIRED CORPORATE IMAGES

After making the decision to embark on a program to change the image of an organisation, the temptation is to outsource the project to a group of experts. The most typical candidates are corporate identity or corporate image consultancies, an advertising agency, or a public relations firm. There are three good reasons however for keeping control of the project in-house.

First, as Figure 6.3 illustrates, the vision, formal policies and organisational culture are often more important than advertising, corporate identity and brand image in designing a new corporate image. And, it is only (senior) managers who can identify and change these. Second, managers and employees are the biggest stakeholders in this type of change program, and they must have 'buy-in' for it to be successful. Third, many internal stakeholders *hate* external consultants taking control.

A good way to manage corporate image change is to form an Image Management Team (IMT) comprised of the CEO and senior managers from human resources, marketing, production and strategic planning. Early on in the project, it is sometimes worthwhile to invite an outside expert in to address this group, outlining a staged approach to change and some (un)successful cases. As the need arises, this group can then outsource market research, identity design, advertising and so forth to professional service providers. But the IMT are the architects and control the change program. Figure 6.4 suggests a process for enhancing an organisation's desired corporate image and thus its reputation.

RECAP

This chapter outlines a new approach to thinking about corporate super-brands. They are defined as a reputation superior to that of

Figure 6.4 The change process

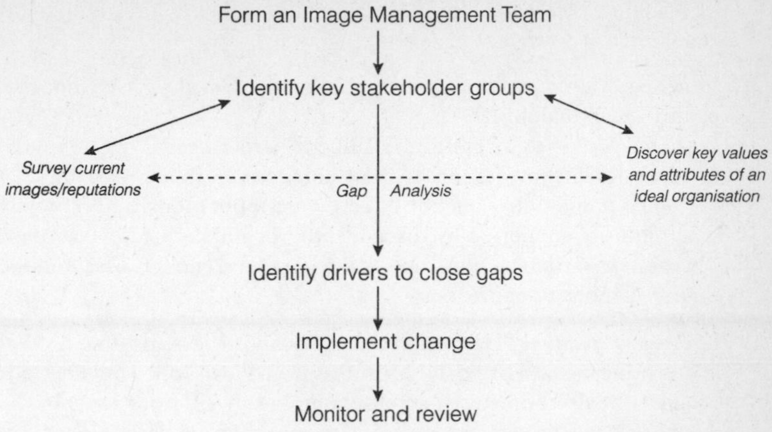

most other companies against which its owner competes. This corporate reputation is a strategic asset that is difficult for other companies to emulate. It thus enables its owner to boost its marketing effectiveness, and to use it as a performance bond when negotiating with other parties.

When an organisation becomes a super-brand, this status acts like a flywheel. It provides a constant stream of energy to the operations of the organisation. All organisations have reputations, however, what differentiates the super-brands from the also-brands is that thc former actively design their flywheel and then proactively manage their strategic asset.

FURTHER READING

D. Bernstein, *Company Image and Reality*, Cassell, London, 1984.
This is an old book that has maintained its relevance quite well. It is written in a journalistic style and thus its ideas are easy to relate to. What it lacks is any supporting evidence for the ideas presented. Hence, you either like it or you don't.

C. Chajet and T. Shachtman, *Image by Design*, Addison-Wesley, Reading, MA, 1991.
This book is a good example of what is available from corporate image design firms—a loose organising framework illustrated by many

corporate examples. To my mind, the 'problem' with books written by corporate design consultants is that the role of corporate design is given more prominence in the corporate reputation development process than it warrants.

G.R. Dowling, *Corporate Reputations*, Longman Cheshire, Melbourne/ Kogan Page, London, 1994.
This is my book—so by definition I like its structure. Its two strengths are that (1) it provides an overall integrating framework for the development and enhancement of corporate reputations, and (2) many of the ideas are supported by research studies and corporate examples. Its weakness is that it does not make a strong enough case for the value of corporate reputations.

C.J. Fombrun, *Reputation*, Harvard Business School Press, Boston, 1996.
This is a big book written by a professor at New York University. It contains a wealth of material across a number of different areas in the private and public sectors. Its primary weakness is that it does not provide an overarching framework for developing and/or managing corporate reputations.

W. Olins, *Corporate Identity*, Harvard Business School Press, Boston, 1989.
This is probably the 'classic' book in the area of corporate identity design. While it is titled *Corporate Identity*, Wally Olins discusses corporate culture and corporate image as much as he does corporate identity. The book is heavily illustrated, which brings many of the ideas to life.

Much of the future research in this area is likely to appear in the new journal *Corporate Reputation Review* (Henry Stewart Publications). This journal publishes a mix of academic papers and case studies of best practice.

7

Schumpeter and the dynamics of firm strategy

PETER W. ROBERTS

Strategy researchers have come to understand that a valid understanding of sustained superior profitability must come to terms with two related questions: 'Where do relatively high profits come from?' and 'What factors operate in favour of (and against) their persistence?'. Arguably, the original work of Joseph Schumpeter provides answers to both of these questions:

> Schumpeter's analysis of how the capitalist engine works recognizes . . . the lure and reward for innovation in the quasi rents from a private temporary monopoly. However, in Schumpter's analysis, the monopoly normally is limited and temporary. Sooner or later, competitors will be able to imitate, or even invent around, or develop a better version of, the initial innovation.[1]

Schumpeter's thinking has grounded numerous attempts to understand the dynamics of innovation, competition and firm profitability. Dennis Mueller makes explicit reference to Schumpeter in discussing the persistence of firm-level profitability, while resource-based theorists have made several references to Schumpeter's 'process of creative destruction' in trying to understand how sustainable competitive advantage may be built and destroyed within dynamic environments.[2] Elsewhere, Richard Nelson and Sydney Winter frame their evolutionary theory of economic change in Schumpeterian terms.[3] Finally, an impressive volume of empirical research has addressed the twin Schumpeterian hypotheses concerning the relationship between innovation and firm size and market structure.[4]

SCHUMPETER'S PROFIT DYNAMICS

Schumpeter set out to distinguish static economics from that which is inherently dynamic. The static component (over-emphasised in both economic and strategy research) entails analysing the economics of the 'circular flow', wherein managers marshal available resources according to established production functions. The price competition that prevails ensures that given sufficient time, an equilibrium results wherein each resource is paid according to its marginal productivity. To Schumpeter, the emphasis on price competition that dominates static economic theory misses a decidedly more important type of competition:

> it is not [price competition] which counts but the competition from the new commodity, the new technology, the new source of supply, the new type of organization . . . competition which commands a decisive cost or quality advantage and which strikes not at the margins of the profits and the outputs of the existing firms but at their foundations and very lives.[5]

In this more dynamic type of competition, entrepreneurs introduce innovations. In doing so they upset the prevailing pattern of exchange, moving markets into disequilibrium positions.[6] In terms of profitability, the crucial fact is that 'the carrying out of new combinations means . . . the different employment of the economic system's existing supplies of productive means'.[7] In order to innovate, the entrepreneur obtains productive factors at prices that correspond to values in the existing circular flow. If successful, the re-deployment of these factors in novel endeavours generates returns that exceed factor costs. This difference between revenues and costs represents the profit to the entrepreneur. As such, by responding to perceived opportunities, successful entrepreneurs earn profits.[8]

A second dynamic is found in Schumpeter's writing, namely an imitative dynamic: '[the entrepreneur] also leads in the sense that he draws other producers in his branch after him . . . they are his competitors, who first reduce and then annihilate his profit'.[9] As this suggests, the economic system does not react passively to above-normal profits. Unless otherwise deterred, imitators arise to compete away the profits earned by the innovator. In the extreme, imitation is immediate and the profit earned by the entrepreneur vanishes almost as soon as it arises; high profits never persist. However, Schumpeter alludes to two factors that might sustain the profits associated with innovation: friction in the competitive mechanisms and the establishment of monopoly positions. Only in an abstract world does competitor imitation operate independent of time. In practice competition does not act promptly and hence enterprises remain in possession of surpluses for considerable periods of time.[10]

For current purposes, we may summarise Schumpeter's competitive process as follows. Above-normal profits are generated as a result of successful innovation and provide an incentive for imitation. To varying degrees, this imitation increases competition levels which erode the profits flowing to the innovator. At one extreme, imitation is unimpeded and the above-normal profits vanish almost instantly. At the other extreme, an innovation is virtually inimitable, generating monopoly returns for the innovator that persist indefinitely.

SCHUMPETER AND THE DYNAMICS OF FIRM STRATEGY

While strategy scholars are beginning to address the dynamic aspects of competition, the majority of the (empirical) work on profit dynamics is found within the industrial organisation economics literature, wherein firm-level profit dynamics have been studied since the mid-1970s.[11] These researchers have moved beyond traditional cross-sectional analyses of profitability as cross-sectional analysis does not provide insights into the dynamic processes that characterise competition. This is seen clearly by distinguishing questions regarding the existence of abnormal profits from those regarding their persistence. It is not problematic from an efficiency perspective that above-normal profits are generated by firms since 'markets have inbuilt error correction mechanisms that function to bid away excess profits'.[12] However, when such mechanisms malfunction (or are pre-empted), abnormal profits may persist, perhaps indefinitely. It is this latter phenomenon that interests persistent profitability scholars.

Following Mueller's seminal work, other researchers turned their attention to the persistent profitability question, each using slightly different methods and/or different samples. While it is difficult to distill consistent themes from a diverse range of empirical studies, the overall impression is that it is typical for high firm-level profits to erode over time. However, the evidence also points to several firms which have been shielded from the imitative competition which otherwise erodes high profit positions. These firms earn high profits over prolonged periods of time and motivate interest in understanding the causes of firm-level persistent profitability.

Within the strategy literature, a focused, theory-based dialogue on the sustained superior performance question is a relatively recent phenomenon. The most obvious example is the ongoing exposition of the resource-based view of the firm, in which sustained superior profitability is related to the resources and capabilities possessed by firms. The basic premise is that firms are heterogeneous with respect to the resources and capabilities that they possess. In a cross-section, firms experience performance differentials because their resources are differentially valuable and rare; with rare meaning, valuable resources yielding superior performance. Moreover, such differences may persist over time. Firms that sustain superior performance of their rare and valuable resources are also inimitable.[13]

A review of the resource-based literature finds numerous references to Schumpeter. For the most part, these citations link resource-base theory with Schumpeter's process of creative destruction. However, Conner finds similarities between resource-based theory and Schumpeterian competition: both suggest that above-normal returns result from new ways of competing; both place entrepreneurial vision at the heart of the firm; and both recognise the potential for competitor imitation.[14] Similarly, Rumelt builds on Schumpeter's ideas by explicitly placing entrepreneurial vision at the heart of a firm's ability to generate abnormal profits.[15] He also stresses the importance of isolating mechanisms, which protect the high profits associated with entrepreneurial discovery.

Although a defining characteristic of resource-based theory is an emphasis on resources as determinants of firm profitability, Schumpeter locates cause in the firm's evolving portfolio of innovations. We should therefore reconcile an apparent inconsistency between Schumpeter and resource-based theory. Note that resource-based logic suggests that resources lead to sustainable competitive advantage which, in turn, yields sustained superior profitability. Competitive advantage implies an ability to deliver products or services that have either a differentiation or a cost advantage relative to competing offerings. In all cases, a competitive advantage must be traced to an innovation on the part of the firm. With a differentiation advantage, the firm introduces a product or service that is superior to available alternatives; its profits are the result of a product innovation. With a cost advantage, the firm uncovers some way to deliver the same product or service at lower cost. Its profits result from some other form of innovation; that is, a new production process, organisational form, or a lower cost source of supply. Finally, these advantages are maintained only as long as competitors are unable to imitate the innovations.

SUMMARY

Researchers and managers alike now fully appreciate the dynamic environments within which firms compete. In light of this, we must reflect on the conceptual adequacy of the strategic frameworks that guide managerial thought and practice. Strategic thinking in the 1970s and 1980s benefited from a foundation built on static economic theories. However, the emerging appreciation of competitive dynamics makes those theories less relevant. In this respect, knowledge of the original writings of Joseph Schumpeter—who first articulated the importance of the twin dynamic processes of innovation and imitation—is highly beneficial to those researchers who are interested in developing new strategic frameworks. It is also critical for managers whose firms' success depends on the effective application of these emerging frameworks.

FURTHER READING

This article provides a brief summary of the contributions made by Joseph Schumpeter to dynamic strategy thinking. Interested readers might consult the abovementioned articles by Kathleen Conner and Richard Rumelt. Space permitting we could have gone on and located Schumpeter's influence in other contemporary strategy perspectives, including Richard D'Aveni's *Hypercompetition* (Free Press, New York, 1994) or Gary Hamel and C.K. Prahalad's *Competing for the Future* (Harvard Business School Press, Boston, 1996). To varying degrees, each of these frameworks owes a common debt to Schumpeter's original thinking on competitive dynamics, which places primary emphasis on the twin dynamic processes of innovation and competitor imitation.

8

Defending market share against a new entrant

JOHN H. ROBERTS, CHARLIE J. NELSON AND PAMELA D. MORRISON

Management libraries are full of books about how to develop and launch new products (for example, Urban and Hauser).[1] The management of innovations is a booming industry in its own right. However, there are two strategic imperatives for any company: to grow by launching new products and invading new markets, and to defend the customers it has.[2] Market defence has attracted very little attention despite the fact that for every new product and innovation launched, there is an incumbent with an existing product that has to develop a strategy to minimise the damage inflicted on it. Defence against competitors' new products poses an important problem and the issues facing the defendant are different to those facing the new entrant. The defendant has four strategic opportunities to reduce the harm done to it by an invading innovation. They are summarised in Figure 8.1. For a study of the prevalence of these strategies see Gatignon et al.[3]

This article looks at ways in which a firm can gain competitive advantage through each of the boxes in Figure 8.1 by looking at an

Figure 8.1 The defendant's strategic challenge

	Enhance and communicate own strengths	Exploit and expose entrant's weaknesses
Ultimate new product appeal	Positive strategies	Negative strategies
Rate at which new product gains share	Retarding strategies	Inertial strategies

application of defence against a new entrant in a Pacific Rim telecommunications market. It builds on the static defence model of Hauser and Shugan[4] by introducing dynamics and calibrating the effect of defensive moves.

CONCEPTUAL FRAMEWORK

To address the strategic challenge set out above, the defending company needed forecasts of the ultimate appeal of the new entrant, its trajectory to that appeal, and the determinants that would influence the equilibrium share and the rate at which it was realised. In calibrating the market prior to the launch of the new entrant, our market research taught us quite a lot about strategies available to defendants. The incumbent firm was a state-owned telecommunications monopoly that was being attacked by a multinational conglomerate. The battleground was the heavy calling segment of the residential long distance market. Focus groups gave us a good feel for the decision process that consumers would go through and that is outlined in Figure 8.2.

Market research was able to estimate the number of consumers who would consider the new entrant, how many of those would try

Figure 8.2 Detailed model of the stages of consumer adoption

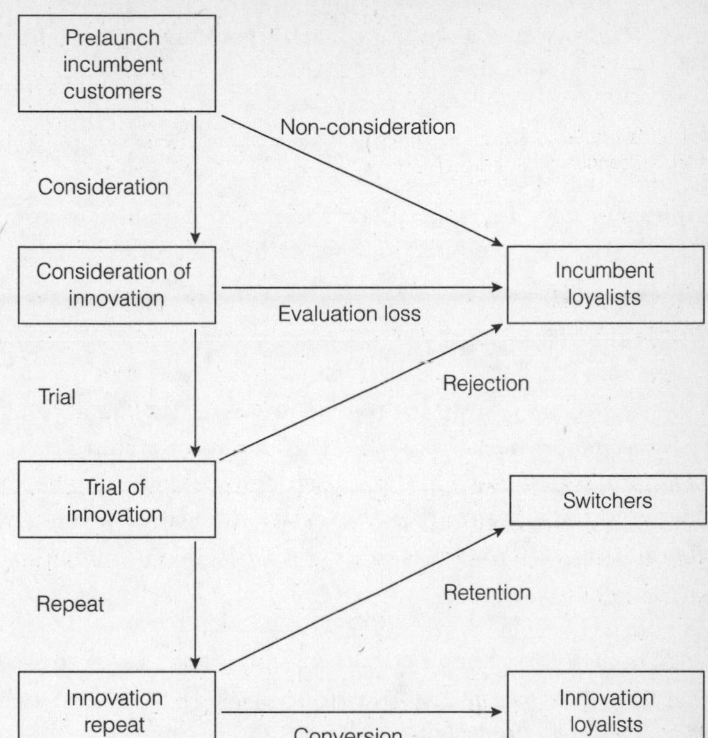

it, whether they would repeat or not, and, given repeat, if they would stay loyal to the new entrant. Not only were the equilibrium shares able to be calculated, but also the rate at which those shares would occur and the determinants of the shares.

MODEL OF ADOPTION BEHAVIOUR

The technique used to understand the market dynamics was macro flow models which specified the behavioural states that consumers will go through in their decision process (see, for example, Urban and Hauser[5] or Hauser and Wisniewski[6]).

The discrete choice model used to calibrate the extent of each of the flows in Figure 8.2 was a binary logic model. Thus each of the relative flows from prelaunch to consider/not consider, from consider to trial/evaluation loss, from trial to repeat/rejection and from repeat to switcher/innovation loyalist could be modelled using the following formulation:

$$P_1 = \frac{_e u_1}{_e u_1 + _e u_2} \qquad (1)$$

where P_1 is the probability of flowing to state 1 and U_1 and U_2 are the utilities of state 1 and state 2, respectively. These state utilities may be further decomposed into the utilities of their constituent attributes:

$$U_j = \sum_k w_k y_{jk} \quad \text{for } j = 1, 2 \qquad (2)$$

where y_{jk} is the amount of attribute k possessed by state j and w_k is the importance of attribute k. This approach follows that of Hauser and Wisniewski.[7] Flow rates can be modeled using geometric decay functions and their associated negative exponential distributions, as follows:

$$F_t = 1 - e^{-\lambda t} \qquad (3)$$

where F_t is the proportion of consumers that have flowed to state 1 and state 2 at each stage by time t, and λ is the flow rate. Again this is the formulation proposed by Hauser and Wisniewski[8] although they also suggest a compound Poisson distribution. Roberts, Nelson and Morrison also fit a Bass model of which the negative exponential is a subset, known as the Fourt and Woodlock model.[9]

Combining equations (1) and (3) gives the expected proportion of the population that has flowed to any given state and Roberts, Nelson and Morrison show that this seven state, eight flow model has a closed form solution.[10] The algebraic specification of the model allows measures to be developed for each of the variables and its parameters to be calibrated.

Numbers flowing ultimately to each stage (the number of considerers, triallists and so forth) were estimated using discrete choice models (see, for example, Roberts and Lilien).[11] For consumers in each behavioural state the model estimated how many would flow to each of the subsequent states and how quickly they would flow. In the market research, respondents were taken through a learning process where they were first told about the new entrant, and then gradually educated about it with simulated advertisements and other material. That enabled us to calculate consumer beliefs about the new entrant at the different stages of knowledge that would occur as the market evolved.

Results

The primary driver of choice of the new entrant was attitudes towards the defendant and also beliefs about what the new player would be like. That is, the first lesson we learned in the market research, and one that all defendants must understand, was that the criteria that are used to judge the new entrant will be different to those used to judge the incumbent. Thus, focus groups indicated fourteen attributes which were important in judging the defendant which could be boiled down using principal components factor analysis to three underlying dimensions: 'How strong is our relationship with the defendant?'; 'What do we believe of its service delivery?'; and 'Do we see it as big and impersonal?'. In contrast, attitudes to the new entrant and the idea of competition were measured on nine separate attributes which could be distilled down to: 'Is there a downside?'; 'Am I restless with my existing supplier?'; 'Do I have a high level of inertia to change?'; and 'Do I care about competition?'. The first three of these factors provide the means by which the defendant can adopt positive strategies in the strategy matrix above to improve its long-term equilibrium/long-term appeal. The bottom four factors enable the defendant to understand how it can use negative strategies to exploit and expose the entrant's weaknesses. It should be pointed out, however, that these negative strategies are not without some risk. With the advent of MCI and Sprint into the US telecommunications market, AT&T tried negative advertising suggesting that new entrants would not be able to match its technological sophistication. These campaigns backfired badly. Having understood the criteria that consumers would use to judge the defendant and the new entrant, we then looked at the determinants as to how people would flow through the decision process outlined above. The determinants of each stage of the process are outlined in Figure 8.3.

Consideration could be reduced if the defendant improved

Figure 8.3 Pre-launch calibration of flow models

Consideration model: 'I would consider the new entrant'

Determinants	Effect
Good relationship with incumbent	–
Service delivery of incumbent good	–
No downside to change	+
Restless with incumbent	+++
High inertia to change	– –

Trial model: 'I would try the new entrant'

Determinants	Effect
Relative price of incumbent	+++
Relative price squared	–
New entrant price plan	+
Defendant price plan	–
Restless with incumbent	+

Repeat model: 'Given satisfactory trial, I would repeat'

Determinants	Effect
Relative price of incumbent	+++
Relative price squared	–
New entrant price plan	+
Defendant price plan	–
Incumbent is big and impersonal	+
No downside to change	+
High inertia to change	+

Conversion model: 'I would still use the incumbent'

Determinants	Effect
Relative price of incumbent	– –
Relative price squared	+
New entrant price plan	–
Defendant price plan	+
Incumbent is big and impersonal	– –
No downside to change	–
High inertia to change	+
Competition is irrelevant	–

service delivery and developed a closer relationship with its customers. Consideration could also be contained if the defendant was able to communicate that there was indeed a downside to switching carrier (particularly since the new entrant was not going to provide a full service offering) or if the defendant could reduce the level of restlessness of consumers. The most interesting point about the pricing which was significant in both the trial and repeat models was that the price sensitivity for the defendant was higher than the price sensitivity for the new entrant. Thus, a price decrease from the new entrant would be more valued than a price decrease by the defendant. If the defendant got into a price war it would be hit by a double whammy: firstly, its margins would be eroded and, secondly, even if it was able to maintain price parity or a similar price differential relative to the new entrant, it would gain a lower share as price decreased. (Of course, it does not follow that it is in the interests of the new entrant to start a price war since its margins would also be eroded.) Note that, trial given, the consumer will consider the new entrant is primarily driven by price (and also restlessness with the defendant). It is interesting to observe that inertia which serves to slow repeat, and thus acts in favour of the defendant, becomes a liability once repeat has occurred since the respondent can now no longer be bothered to keep on continuing to use the existing carrier.

Originally the defendant thought that the best place to erect inertial strategies was to try to persuade the consumer that there was no need to try the new entrant. These data show that in fact inertia may well be most effectively employed after trial has occurred, and this came as a surprising finding to management. The best line of defence in fact was not at consideration but after having let the consumer try the product to just let it fade out of his or her mind. Finally, the conversion model to stop the consumers who repeat with the new entrant from staying with it totally, could be influenced by decreasing the consumer perception that the incumbent carrier was arrogant and insensitive.

These strategies all provided good ammunition to contain the market share that the new entrant would gain. A further requirement was to understand the rate at which the new entrant would gain that share. We addressed that problem in two ways. First, this new entrant had invaded other markets and so we were able to fit a diffusion model to see its past progress in foreign markets and by analogy to estimate its likely progress in this market. Second, we asked respondents how long they thought it would take them to make a decision about the new entrant. Remarkably, the migration rates from these very different methods proved to be almost identical (see Mahajan, Muller and Bass[12] for a review of calibrating such diffusion models). Because we had self-stated migration rates, we could see the different consumer characteristics that fast and slow migrations rates were associated with. By looking at the determinants that would lead to consumers changing quickly to the new entrant we were able to see how that could possibly be slowed. The determinants of conversion are included in Figure 8.4.

Speeding up the conversion rate are consumers' perceptions that the defendant is not responsive to their needs and also a resentment of the defendant. Slowing the migration rate down is a perception that there is no real reason to change to the new entrant (except perhaps to save money) and also that maybe it would not be as good. These strategies, the third and fourth boxes of the strategic challenge matrix in Figure 8.1, are potentially very effective in slowing down the rate of diffusion. While AT&T was not highly successful at reducing the equilibrium appeal of new entrants, one area where it did have a very successful campaign was with its inertial strategies. One of the advertising campaigns of AT&T had copy along the lines of 'When our competitors call you up and offer you substantial savings on your telephone bill, don't believe them. Get it in writing'. The beauty of this strategy was that it made the whole conversion process just that much more difficult. It was intuitive to customers in that it made sense to get the promise of savings in writing, but it also made the whole process a substantial hassle. Many consumers deferred doing anything about it. The drivers of inertial strategies proved to be an extremely useful way to buoy up the defendant's share.

The forecasts which came out of this prelaunch model proved to be extremely accurate (within 1 per cent of the actual market share for the first six months of the new entrant's operation). They were also extremely diagnostic. By tackling the problem of dynamic defence against a new entrant, we were able to pick up the different

Figure 8.4 Relationship between flow rate and inertial variables

Determinant of high conversion speeds	Effect
The defendant is not responsive to my needs	+
I'd use the new entrant to teach the defendant a lesson	+
Saving money is the only reason to use the new entrant	–
Using the new entrant might be risky	– –

criteria that consumers use to evaluate the defendant and the new entrant. That way the defendant could compete on grounds that favoured it. We were able to identify the real danger of a price war because of the extra margin loss, larger base to which that loss would be applied, and bigger response effect. We found out the sustainability of a defence strategy post-trial, based on the very high expectations of a new entrant. Finally, we discovered that service of the defendant had a dual role. First, we found that perceived service levels affected how the defendant was perceived. Second, and perhaps more interestingly, we found that perceptions of the new entrant could be changed dramatically by changing perceptions of the defendant. Any improvements in service perceptions carried with them this double bonus. More details of both the model and results obtained in applying it are contained in Roberts, Nelson and Morrison.[13]

IMPLICATIONS FOR MANAGEMENT ACTION

Managers face new entrants with increasing frequency. This research points to a number of areas where they can take action that will protect their customer base and ensure that damage to their bottom line is minimised. The first and most obvious action is the gathering of good market intelligence. If the incumbent does not know the competition (its strengths, where it will attack, who it will attack and so on) and the customers (their perceptions of the incumbent's strengths and weaknesses, their preference drivers and so on) then any focus to defensive strategies can only be well-targeted by chance. The second action is that the incumbent gets the business basics right. No communication strategy, no matter how compelling, offers long-term protection for a firm that is not providing the product at a service level consistent with customer expectations. The research shows that service standards affect customers in two ways. First, and as expected, they drive the perceived utility of the incumbent. Second, and more subtly, they drive the perceived utility of the new entrant. Put differently, high service levels will offer a positive weapon for the incumbent and an Achilles heel for the entrant. Poor service levels provide the converse. Armed with good intelligence and an action plan in place to address the business basics the incumbent can erect a number of other defence barriers. It can understand the consumer decision process and work out where to erect preference and inertial barriers (in our case it was post-trial). It can understand the different drivers of incumbent and new entrant utility and fight on a battleground that best suits its response functions (in our case it was advertising rather than price). And it can choose who to fight over using its information advantage of existing customers to differentially defend market segments. To do less than this is to surrender unnecessary territory and shareholder value.

CONCLUSION

Large, strong and mature organisations spend a lot of time thinking about their growth strategies. In doing so, many of them get blind-sided by assuming they will hang on to what they have. Similarly, academics and consultants have spent much time understanding new products and growth strategies. They have spent little time considering how to combat them.

There are very strong and viable ways in which a company can defend its existing turf. It must understand the advantages it enjoys against the new entrant as well as the disadvantages. It must move the battle to ground where it can exploit those advantages. For example, if a defendant with a market share of 90 per cent devotes 1 per cent of its revenue to advertising against a new entrant with a 10 per cent share which is also devoting 1 per cent of its revenue to advertising, then the defendant can gain a share of voice of nine times that of the new entrant. Obviously, the defendant must have something worthwhile to say, but advertising represents an area where the defendant's size works for it, while pricing represents an area where the defendant's size works against it. By understanding the battleground, that is, the consumer, the defendant can embark upon highly successful marketing warfare against any attacking force. Without such an understanding it is impossible for the incumbent organisation to focus its defensive forces to areas where they will be most effective.

FURTHER READING

G. Day, *Market Driven Strategy: Processes for Creating Value*, The Free Press, New York, 1990.
This text provides an excellent overview of setting marketing strategy. It provides the framework in which defence takes place for the firm.

H. Gatignon, T.S. Robertson and A.J. Fein, 'Incumbent Defense Strategies against New Product Entry', *International Journal of Research in Marketing*, 14, May, 1997, pp. 163–76.
This paper provides a survey overview of the different types of defensive marketing strategies being adopted by firms.

J.R. Hauser, and S.M. Shugan, 'Defensive Marketing Strategies', *Marketing Science*, 2, 4, 1983, pp. 319–60.
Hauser and Shugan's piece is a theoretical one. It determines the conditions under which a defending firm should increase or decrease marketing expenditure to maximise its profit.

J.R. Hauser and K. Wisniewski, 'Application, Predictive Test and Strategy Implications for a Dynamic Model of Consumer Response', *Marketing Science*, 1, Spring, 1982, pp. 143–79.
This paper outlines an approach to calibrating defensive strategies by looking at how consumers will flow through different decision stages.

V. Mahajan, E. Muller and F.M. Bass, 'New Product Diffusion Models in Marketing: A Review and Directions for Research', *Journal of Marketing*, 54, January, 1990, pp. 1–26.
Diffusion models have been extremely popular in marketing to describe the dynamics of new product diffusion. New products are seen to spread through the population analogously to diseases in epidemiology. This paper provides an excellent survey of that literature.

J.H. Roberts and G.L. Lilien, 'Explanatory and Predictive Models of Consumer Behavior' in *Handbooks in Operations Research and Management*

Science: Marketing, vol. 5, edited by J. Eliashberg and G.L. Lilien, North Holland, Amsterdam, 1993.
Eliashberg and Lilien's book provides an overview of different approaches to modeling phenomena in the marketplace, with different chapters devoted to different aspects of marketing theory, each written by experts in the field. This chapter provides a summary of the different approaches in marketing to assessing and harnessing different stages in the consumer decision process.

J.H. Roberts, C.J. Nelson and P.D. Morrison, 'Defending Market Share Against an Emerging Innovation', Working Paper 95-006 April, 1995, Australian Graduate School of Management, University of New South Wales, Kensington.
The problem of defence addressed by this chapter is described in more technical detail in the Roberts, Nelson and Morrison paper referenced here. That paper provides the mathematics and more detailed results of the application.

G.L. Urban and J.R. Hauser, *Design and Marketing of New Products*, 2nd edn, Prentice Hall, Englewood Cliffs, NJ, 1993.
Market defence strategies are erected as a reaction to new products entering the market. An excellent summary of the approaches that new products are likely to take and how to calibrate their effects is provided in this text.

9

The effective leadership of corporate change

DENNIS TURNER

When I try and summarise what I've learned since 1981 one of the big lessons is that change has no constituency. People like the status quo. They like the way it was. When you start changing things, the good old days look better and better. You've got to be prepared for massive resistance.

—Jack Welch, CEO, General Electric

Campbell's people had incredible pride. When I drew attention to the fact that their results sucked then, man, I stirred up a hornet's nest of very proud talented people. They wanted to win as badly as I did.

—David Johnson, CEO, Campbell Soup Company

When I come in, I like to make change very quickly.

—Al Dunlap, Chainsaw

One thing Girraween [a Du Pont plant in Sydney which achieved significant successful change] taught us is you can't do things quickly.

—Dick Warburton, then Managing Director, Du Pont (Australia) Limited

Most guidance, knowledge and insight about corporate change is largely anecdotal. We read how Paul Simons in Australia revitalised Woolworths or how in America, Jack Welch changed General Electric or Jan Carlzon in Europe changed SAS (Scandinavian Airlines System). The many battle stories, sometimes written by the generals, make fascinating reading. Amongst the often conflicting conclusions they draw there are real pearls of wisdom. But which are the real pearls and which the artificial ones? On what basis can you make a judgment?

IS EVERY CHANGE DIFFERENT?

Not only are there differing views on how to achieve successful change but the changes that organisations try to achieve also vary enormously. Some focus on changing culture, others on introducing new technologies. Some involve new alliances, or new product developments, others focus on contraction or cost reduction. Yet others alter structures, or focus on changing top management. And change is as endemic and important in small organisations as in large, in the public sector as in the private sector.

MANAGEMENT ACTION TO MEET THREE FUNDAMENTAL NEEDS

However, whilst each change is indeed in some respects unique, our research into 243 cases of corporate change in Australia and New Zealand shows there are some fundamental capabilities that underlie effective management actions which are strongly linked to change success across varied changes and situations.[1] To be effective in achieving change, management action must achieve three things:

1 the *engagement* of the people of the organisation in the change;
2 the *development* of the resources of the organisation to meet the needs of the change; and
3 the simultaneous *performance management* of both the change process and the ongoing operations.

These three fundamental and essential needs for effective corporate change provide a clear, sharp framework and strong focus for action by those who wish to lead their organisations successfully through change. However, action is needed not only at the top or by the few but, to achieve significant change, action is needed by the many, across and throughout the organisation. As we discuss below, such action is facilitated and strengthened by the existence of corporate capabilities in engagement, development and performance management and the way the 'state' of the organisation is managed throughout the change

What makes management actions work?

Action can be effective or ineffective. Many attempted corporate changes fail. Indeed much evidence, including our own research, is that many more fail to achieve their objectives than fully succeed. Successful action, in any field, rests ultimately on underlying capability. For example, most readers of this chapter would have driven to work this morning. You got into your car at home. When you stepped out of it at work it is likely that you would have forgotten the hundreds of actions you took to arrive safely at work. By now you have developed and internalised a capability in driving. That capability enabled you to take many actions in different situations and under varying pressures. You take action every time you get into your car, but the effectiveness of those actions depends on your fundamental capability as a driver.

Without capability, you can take action in a situation and be lucky once or twice. But to perform over time you must have capability in what the activity or task needs for success. When you have this, you know what is important to performance, where to focus effort, how best to use your resources, how to time your action and how to integrate the knowledge and skills you have to achieve your aim. And you can produce, repeat or vary your actions in different situations and under pressure and still maintain high performance standards.

For example, if we looked at management actions at Woolworths, Du Pont's Giraween Sydney plant, the NSW State Library, and StorageTek, all of whom made very successful changes in recent years, we would see very different actions and emphases.

While action to reposition the firm in the marketplace was central to Woolworths and StorageTek it was not to Du Pont. Though Woolworths sought staff stability, an end to frequent job rotation, and a focus on personal specialisation, the State Library moved towards less specialisation and changes in culture and structure. While StorageTek built its entry into a new market with specialised external senior recruitment, Woolworths achieved its success with a team composed almost entirely of insiders. Though training was a factor in all changes, in some it focused on acquiring new technical skills, yet in others it was focused on personal growth. In some the training was entirely voluntary, in others compulsory. In some cost reduction was very important, in others it was not. At Du Pont, trade union action in developing a 'joint beliefs statement' with the management was the initial key to success but union cooperation or centrality was not evident in any of the other examples.

Although these actions were appropriate and worked for the organisations concerned, looked at in themselves they give little basis for generalised advice. Seen as particular manifestations of the more fundamental underlying capabilities of *engagement* or *development* or *performance management*, their importance and contribution as part of the successful changes is clear.

But while these organisations were making effective change they also had to manage their ongoing business. You cannot close your organisation down while you change it for the future. So organisations need to have the skills and take actions to simultaneously manage both corporate change and current performance. Are these the same? Or does managing corporate change require different actions and skills from those needed to manage current performance?

RESEARCH FINDINGS—MANAGING CHANGE AND PERFORMANCE

Research into 243 cases of change in Australian and New Zealand organisations enables us to identify a structure of five essential capabilities which underlie effective management action to enable a firm to meet the two requirements of long-term performance; that is, to perform well at any point of time and yet to be able to change effectively whenever change is needed.[2]

Capabilities exist as the personal capabilities of managers in the business and as corporate capabilities of the organisation itself. The capabilities not only provide the necessary base for effective action but also identify the areas where that effective action will be needed.

The five essential capabilities for long-term performance

We identified five essential capabilities for long-term performance. The five capabilities split into two fundamental groupings. One group, *reshaping capabilities*, enables an organisation to change effectively. The second group, *operational capabilities*, provides the basis for current performance and results. Each of the two groups consists of three capabilities since one capability, performance management, is common to both groups. Figure 9.1 shows the essential dynamics of the performance and change processes.

Our data strikingly show that the capabilities to achieve effective change are very different from those needed to achieve current business performance. A business needs both these two differing

Figure 9.1 Dynamics of the performance and change processes

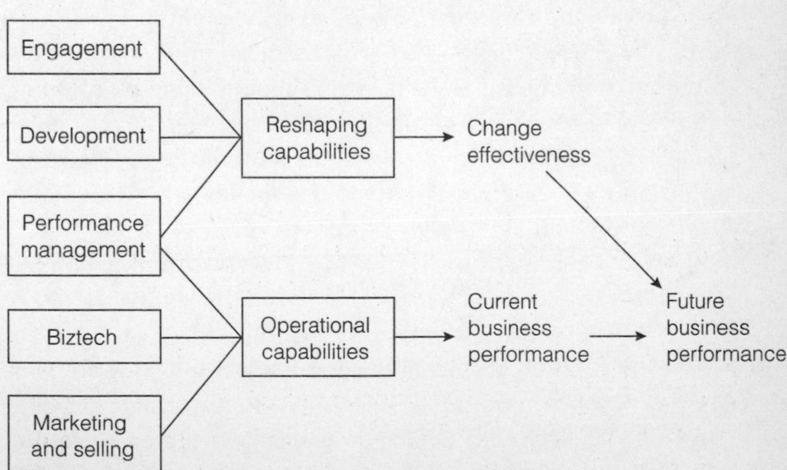

sets of capabilities if it is to achieve long-term performance. Having one set of capabilities is not related to having the other. Being good at running a business today has little relationship to the ability to change it, and vice versa. Performance management is the one capability which contributes significantly to both operational performance and change effectiveness.

Reshaping capabilities

Three capabilities provide the basis for action to achieve effective change. These are, *engagement*, *development* and *performance management*. These capabilities are needed by organisations *whenever* change is needed. The first, engagement, is about getting the members throughout the organisation informed, involved, committed and motivated to act to achieve the firm's purpose and future directions. The second, development, involves developing all the resources—personal, physical, technological and systems—needed to achieve the firm's future directions. The third, performance management, involves managing the factors that drive the processes of change. These include not only systems and processes but often changes in behaviour, and sometimes values, embedded in the firm's culture.

Each capability is formed from a number of contributing competencies. For example, the contributing competencies that go to form engagement include those relevant to finding new directions and opportunities and also those needed to get commitment to them. Engagement is much more than communication or motivation, though these are important to it. It is also about having pathfinding skills; developing, crystallising and articulating new directions or strategies to accomplish the purposes and values of the organisation. It is difficult to get real engagement without knowing and being involved in where you are going or likely to go.

Similarly, development capability includes contributing competencies not only in the actual development of all kinds of resources but also in skills in deciding which resources are relevant for the organisation's future directions. Development is not an end in itself but a means to higher future performance. Performance management likewise includes a range of contributing competencies, including resource application, performance control, and financial, planning and integration competencies which combine to form this essential capability.

Action based on the three reshaping capabilities meets two vital needs. It reshapes the organisation's operational capabilities which will, in turn, provide the firm's future performance and results. Second, reshaping actions influence the organisation's state so that a critical mass of its members collectively understand the intended changes, become committed to them, grow confident in their collective abilities to succeed and are empowered to take action. Action, not just talk, is vital to effective change—action across the organisation, not just at the top, or the middle, or at the coal face.

Across the sample of 243 cases of corporate change, as the strength of reshaping capabilities rises, so change success rises. As strength falls, change success falls.

Operational capabilities

Three capabilities provide the basis for action to achieve current business performance. Since these capabilities enable an organisation to perform well at any point in time they are *always* needed. We called these biztech, performance management and marketing and selling.

Biztech consists of competencies involved in commanding and understanding the technologies, processes and mechanisms through which the organisation creates and delivers its products and services to its market. The concept is wider than core technologies, which focus on technical aspects, or core competencies that someone has judged are the most important competencies. It includes all those business technologies and related processes that are needed to provide value to the customer. Marketing and selling lies in understanding, selling and responding to the organisation's markets and customers in the context of the broader external environment. Performance management which, as we have seen, is a strong contributor to change, also influences and drives the organisation's operational processes and performance, to ensure high results are consistently achieved. Operational capabilities are frequently the major base and focus for management action. But having strong operational capabilities does not, generally, help to change your business effectively. Our data shows that high current performance is, at best, a weak predictor of the ability to change.

PERSONAL AND EMBEDDED CORPORATE CAPABILITIES

Capabilities can be personal and embedded. A manager may have personal capabilities in, say, planning or in communicating or in a technical area, such as brand management or logistics. An organisation, similarly, may have a corporate capability in these or any aspect of its business. Corporate capabilities are embedded in the fabric of the organisation, in its practices, processes, systems, structures, culture, values, know-how and technologies. Importantly this is as true for reshaping capabilities as it is for operational ones. Whilst personal capabilities leave the organisation when their owner does, embedded corporate capabilities tend to endure despite the comings and goings of individuals. In *Change Power: Capabilities That Drive Corporate Renewal* (see further reading at the end of this chapter) we describe and illustrate how capabilities are embedded within the organisation.

When an organisation has strong embedded reshaping capabilities, many actions which help to achieve change will take place as part of the normal, typical way in which the organisation works. For example, when an organisation has a strong corporate capability in engagement, actions will take place as part of its normal way of working which will help the people to become engaged in the changes. Likewise, if it is strong in development capability it will take many actions as part of its normal way of operating to develop and change its resources. This is similar for performance management. In many cases new situations will arise which the organisation has not faced before. Nevertheless, the organisation will have in place practices, processes, systems, mechanisms and supporting cultures that will energise and facilitate individual and collective behaviour and action that will provide valuable support for whatever needs to be done.

Where organisations have weak corporate reshaping capabilities, the success of change will depend much more on the personal reshaping capabilities of key individuals. These leaders will have to ensure that actions to achieve engagement, development and performance management are taken throughout the change in a way which impacts on the whole of the organisation. This demands much greater effort and personal skill than when those same capabilities are owned by the organisation itself.

ORGANISATIONAL STATES

The effectiveness of action is not solely a matter of having the necessary capabilities to act. The level of performance is also influenced by the 'state' of the actor, whether an individual or an organisation. For example, our own personal performance is impacted by our state of confidence, or fitness, or sense of self-efficacy, or motivation to succeed. Organisational states—the collective beliefs, feelings, behaviours and prevailing conditions which affect individual and collective action and predisposition to act—are thus important to both change and performance.

Our data enables us to identify a number of organisational states that are linked to successful change and business performance. Some states have stronger impact on change effectiveness and some on current business performance. For example, states of commitment, or understanding, or empowerment, enhance change effectiveness while a state of conflict undermines it. A state of esprit de corps is strongly linked to high business performance.

Management action is needed during change to create the states which help to make the changes successful. Whilst corporate capabilities take time to build, managers can, if they are motivated, take action relatively quickly to help the development of states which enhance effective change and minimise those which make it harder to achieve.

THE EFFECTIVE LEADERSHIP OF CHANGE

The leadership of change is not principally about leaders having charisma, or the personality or style of the chief executive. Although the specific form that action takes will be shaped by the situation, whatever your situation may be, to achieve successful change you need to:

- engage your people in the change to get their understanding and commitment;
- develop the skills, resources, systems and processes needed for the new directions; and
- manage the performance of the change process and of the organisation through change.

The fundamental job in change leadership is to see that engagement, development and performance management actually take place. Simple as this sounds, managers very frequently fail to do this even when they have the skills and recognise the importance of these actions. Often the reason is 'lack of time', but if you do not have the time to change effectively why attempt change? That is just a recipe for damaging morale and wasting resources. Managers worry about 'change burnout'. One of the best ways to achieve change burnout is to repeatedly attempt ineffective change. This damages esprit de corps and trust in management. Change burnout is not primarily a problem of too much change but of too much change done badly.

In attempting change managers frequently seek to make investment in new systems, technologies, processes and tools of different sorts. Put these proposed investments to the fundamental test of asking; 'Will this help to engage our people?'; 'Will this investment help develop the resources and skills and systems needed for our future direction?'; 'Will this assist us to manage our change and renewal more effectively?'; and 'If it does not do any of these, what does it do that is important for our change and renewal?'. Much effort by top management goes into assessing the contribution new interventions and tools supposedly offer before a decision is made, but frequently little or no effort is made to get engagement, or appropriate development, for the critical mass who will need to make them work.

Key areas where top management are in a unique position to make best use of their skills to have the greatest personal impact on effective change are:

- pathfinding, in particular, in the synthesis, integration and crystallisation of future direction;
- setting levels of performance expectations;
- deciding priorities; and
- influencing the direction of development.

But to increase your organisation's ability to deal with future change, developing personal reshaping skills is not enough. You need to embed relevant aspects of the reshaping capabilities in the fabric of the business itself. Such action contributes to the development of those organisational states which enhance change effectiveness and enables an organisation to achieve some real, collective and corporate influence over its own continued renewal and long-term performance.

FURTHER READING

Books

D. Turner and M. Crawford, *Change Power: Capabilities That Drive Corporate Renewal*, Business and Professional Publishing, Sydney, 1998.
An analysis and description, based on large scale research, of the essential capabilities needed for successful corporate change and renewal, and a practical framework and clear guide for effective managerial action.

J.P. Kotter, *Leading Change*, Harvard Business School Press, Boston MA, 1996.
An interesting personal perspective of the reasons why corporate changes so frequently fail and the description of an eight-stage process to avoid the pitfalls and achieve successful change.

J.C. Collins and J.I. Porras, *Built to Last*, HarperBusiness, New York, 1994.
An analysis of the reasons for success of eighteen major US and global corporations who have performed well over very long periods of time and an insightful description of the central part played in this by both enduring corporate vision, values and culture and the development of ambitious goals for change.

N. Tichy and S. Sherman, *Control Your Destiny Or Someone Else Will*, HarperBusiness, New York, 1994.
A very readable account of the work of Jack Welch, CEO of General Electric, in transforming one of America's most important organisations

and the way in which his approach to change and performance developed over more than a decade of his tenure.

Articles

G. Hamel, 'Strategy Innovation and the Quest for Value', *Sloane Management Review*, Winter, 1998, pp. 7–14.
A thought-provoking article that explores how new strategies emerge in organisations and the part played by new voices, new conversations, new passions and new experiments in this process.

D. Teece, G. Pisano and A. Shuen, 'Dynamic Capabilities and Strategic Management', *Strategic Management Journal*, 18, 7, 1997, pp. 509–33.
A review of the part played in performance and change by corporate capabilities and the key role played by strategic management in adapting, integrating and reconfiguring them to match the requirements of a changing environment.

D. Leonard-Barton, 'Core Capabilities: A Paradox in Managing New Product Development', *Strategic Management Journal*, 13, 1992, pp. 111–25.
An exploration of the nature of corporate capabilities and an analysis of both their positive and negative impact on new product and process development.

C.K. Prahalad and G. Hamel, 'The Core Competence of the Corporation', *Harvard Business Review*, May–June, 1990, pp. 79–91.
A seminal article illustrating and describing corporate competencies as the root of competitive performance and the wellspring of new business development.

10

Steps to the future: emerging approaches to IT-based organisational transformation

CHRISTOPHER SAUER

Experience has shown that, to gain new business value through information technology (IT), a company usually requires organisational transformation. Unfortunately it has proved surprisingly hard to replicate the few, well-publicised successes such as SABRE, which shifted American Airlines into the reservation system business, and Oticon, the Danish hearing aid company, which turned itself around by creating a fluid IT-enabled organisation that could respond effectively to market threats. While such successes have demonstrated the potential of IT-based transformation, the majority of businesses have found the results of their efforts have rarely matched the promise.

Fortunately, two new approaches to IT-based transformation are emerging. One defines principles of incrementalism to guide the transformation process. The other defines the competencies organisations require to underpin their transformation efforts. These approaches promise better outcomes because they address the reasons for past failures. They have the potential to be doubly effective because they are complementary not competing.

THE TRADITIONAL MIND-SET—BARRIER TO SUCCESS

A major reason managers have found it so difficult to replicate the successes of American Airlines, Oticon and others can be traced to the mind-set by which those managers and their consultants have approached their task. Quite simply, we have all been too easily dazzled by the elegance of the transformed organisations we have tried to imitate. Consequently, our attention has focused on the final form of the organisation. We have assumed the pioneers who managed the changes we seek to imitate knew where they were going from the outset—that the secret of their success lay in their strategic vision. But all too often they only discovered their destination when they arrived. What made them successful was the process by which they undertook their transformation. The brilliance of their strategic vision is mostly a reconstruction after the fact.[1]

The mind-set underlying traditional IT management principles has encouraged the focus on strategic vision. It takes a highly rational and mechanistic view of organisation and IT. It only takes account of explicit knowledge, downplaying the importance of those hard-to-articulate competencies that constitute the status quo. It leads naturally to the belief that the critical element of transformation is the creative act of designing a radically new strategy, and blueprinting the combination of organisation and technology required to deliver that. The process of transformation has thus come to be defined as a systematic process of following a rational plan that, on paper, links the vision to the starting point.

The traditional mind-set has been persuasive because it is rooted in two popular strands of thought, one business, one technological. In business in the 1980s, Porter's positioning school of strategy dominated senior management thinking. It emphasised strategic vision of where you wanted to position your company. It focused on rational decision-making and de-emphasised the dirty realities of change.

The technological influence in the traditional mind-set derives from the utterly logical character of computer hardware and software. Computers are a rational micro-world in which machine behaviour can be successfully designed and implemented. Technologists spend much of their time constructing systems which follow instructions to the letter. In consequence, they often suppose that the organisational world is similarly rational. Design is therefore viewed as more important than the process of change implementation.

In varying forms, the last decade's three most popular approaches to gaining business value from IT—Strategic Information Systems Planning (SISP), Strategic Alignment, and Business Process Re-engineering (BPR)—have all emphasised strategic design and planning over the change process. BPR has a notoriously low success rate. SISP and Strategic Alignment have had some success in delivering IT support for the existing business but no more than BPR in delivering new business value.

We therefore need to look beyond these popular approaches, which are often regarded as 'best practices'. At the Fujitsu Centre in the Australian Graduate School of Management we have researched the successes of Australian companies which have tried alternative approaches.[2] The two most common alternatives we have seen companies take have been to outsource or to take a more proactive, incremental approach to managing the organisational change process. Outsourcing proves not to be a successful route to IT-based transformation whereas incrementalism is much more promising.

Outsourcing—not a route to transformation

For those companies for which IT is just a commodity, outsourcing has been a commonsense choice. What the outsourcer requires is reliable IT operational services and technology management at market prices. As a professional service provider, the outsourcing supplier can usually deliver these. It is not required to develop technology which will differentiate the outsourcer from its competitors.

For those still hoping IT will provide a competitive advantage, outsourcing is increasingly looking to be an inappropriate option. Notwithstanding much rhetoric about strategic outsourcing partnerships, the reality has been that outsourcers have all too often found that their partners have been unwilling or unable to address the strategic issues. The staged unravelling of General Motors' total outsourcing contract to EDS is just one among many examples which reveal the difficulties of making strategic outsourcing work. Often the decision to outsource has been made so as to avoid the outsourcing company having to invest in new ways of thinking about leveraging IT. Unfortunately for them, the supplier companies have equally not wanted to move away from the traditional mind-set and risk their ability to win and maintain share in the expanding outsourcing market. Thus, in current conditions, outsourcing does not appear a promising route to successful IT-based transformation.

Incrementalism—managing the change process

The second alternative approach has been for businesses to concentrate on their change processes. Such companies have adopted new principles which simplify the management of change and contain its risks. They have pursued small but rapidly achievable business benefits through adapting the organisation in single steps—the approach of incrementalism. The process of transforming the organisation therefore consists of a sequence of distinct organisational changes. Tables 10.1 and 10.2 illustrate the sequences of steps taken by two Australian organisations. For example, in the Sydney architecture firm, Flower and Samios (Table 10.1), step 1 involved technology change, step 2 role and skill changes, step 3 structural change, step 4 management process changes and step 5 strategy change. These examples also show that the practice of incrementalism is applicable to large organisations such as the NSW Roads and Traffic Authority (RTA) as well as to small and medium enterprises (SMEs) like Flower and Samios.

PRINCIPLES FOR SUCCESSFUL TRANSFORMATION

Careful research of examples such as Flower and Samios and the Roads and Traffic Authority (Tables 10.1 and 10.2) reveals a number of the practical principles underlying the incremental approach

Table 10.1 Step-by-step transformation of Flower and Samios Architects

Flower and Samios Architects	
Step	*Contribution to transformation*
1 Architectural software introduced one project at a time until all work is computer-based	Risk minimised by subsuming new technology cost in project cost; improved presentation and accuracy, ease of revision
2 Architects' skills developed and roles adjusted, 3-D design	Functional richness of technology exploited; for example, instant response to client variations, real-time costing; improved client understanding of designs
3 Structural adjustment as draughtspeople become redundant	Organisational simplification and cost savings
4 Computer-based internal communications and accounting processes	Improved coordination and lower cost management
5 Strategic opportunities emerged	Competitive position improved with five-fold growth in portfolio, business positioned to offer new client services and bid for new types of business

Table 10.2 Step-by-step transformation of the NSW Roads and Traffic Authority's registration and licensing business

NSW Roads and Traffic Authority	
Step	*Contribution to transformation*
1 Regionalisation of structure	Moved business closer to its client base
2 Multiskilling of registry staff	Improved customer service at motor registries, staff more easily managed
3 DRIVES registration and licensing system implemented	Provided a 'one-stop-shop' in registries; removed risk of outmoded technology, improved customer service and customer satisfaction
4 New resource deployment processes	DRIVES' management information and multiskilling permit flexible staff allocation to increase efficiency and effectiveness
5 Strategic opportunities emerge	Registration and licensing no longer a problem, opportunity for new initiatives in road safety; for example Safe-T-Cam

(Figure 10.1). Principle 1 is the essence of incrementalism. It mandates that transformation be undertaken through a sequence of small steps.

Figure 10.1 Principles of the incrementalist approach to IT-based transformation

1	Make organisational change one step at a time.
2	Select each step so that it is reinforced by performance gains.
3	Limit risk to one step at a time.
4	Start change from the basis of existing performance competencies.
5	Adopt a bias for action—learn lessons by acting.
6	Develop change competencies in the business and IT.
7	Embed IT in the business—make IT decisions business decisions.
8	Be opportunistic—look for opportunities after each step.

Principle 2 provides a rule of thumb for the selection or design of a step. It requires that each step, as a constituent change in the process of transformation, should deliver some performance benefit to the organisation. This has the simple virtue of improving performance. At the same time, it reinforces the change and thereby helps to embed it as a standard practice. The RTA exemplified this (Table 10.2). Structural change at step 1 moved it closer to its customer base; multiskilling at step 2 improved over-the-counter customer service; technology innovation at step 3 provided a one-stop-shop; new resource deployment processes at step 4 generated efficiency and effectiveness gains; and the strategic shift at step 5 brought improved policing of vehicle safety regulations.

Principle 3 recommends that risk be limited to one step at a time. Where principle 2 requires some performance gains at each step, principle 3 goes further in recommending that the success of steps should be as independent of each other as possible. It has been a common failing in management information systems implementation for performance gains to be dependent on operational users acquiring new skills and adopting new technology to collect the necessary information without any performance advantage for themselves. Principle 3 requires that such management information systems be designed to benefit the operational users as well as the managers. Then, if for any reason the managers choose not to use the system, some performance gain has been made at the operational level.

Principle 4 reminds us to start change from the basis of existing competencies. For example, Flower and Samios introduced computers as an alternative way of drawing designs, a competence their architects all possessed. Although subsequently the architects found they had adopted a radically different way of designing, moving from thinking in 2-D to thinking in 3-D, Flower and Samios did not make the mistake of expecting that the implementation of the technology alone would immediately enable the architects to switch to 3-D design. The architects had to start from a competence they already possessed, and move gradually to the new way of doing things.

Principle 5 enjoins managers to adopt a bias for action. We learn lessons through trying to make change, not by gazing at the strategic drawing board, incessantly trying to improve the organisational blueprint. Initially, this incurs the costs of unsuccessful experimentation. However, if we adopt principles 1 to 4, these costs are minimised.

Principle 6 reflects increasing understanding of the distinctive nature of change competencies. Not only is it necessary to take action to make change, it is necessary for both the business and IT to have competencies to enable organisational change to be successfully undertaken on a continuing basis. This is in stark contrast to the mistaken, though widespread, belief that technology itself is a change agent. Most IT-based change is heavily dependent on the success of associated organisational change. Where managers attend only to the technology change, resistance to IT is common.

Principle 7 is to embed IT in the business, and to make IT decisions business decisions. The Fujitsu Centre's research has found that the businesses that are best able to gain value from IT and to continue innovating successfully with IT are those for which the technology is an integral part of business decision-making. Where IT and business decisions are treated separately there continues to be a gap between IT and business agendas. By contrast, where a single business decision is made which is necessarily informed by the IT issues, it is far easier to ensure that IT delivers value for the business. For example, in many oil companies the specialist seismic interpretation systems are selected, implemented, maintained and managed by the professional geologists who use them. Adoption and use is not a separate technology decision, it is a decision about how the oil companies conduct their exploration business. In such cases, the perennial problem of satisfying business managers about the return from IT dissolves. They only make a positive adoption decision because they are convinced it makes good business sense.

Finally, principle 8 encourages managers to be opportunistic. This is consistent with the shift away from the traditional mind-set's over-emphasis on strategic vision, design, and planning. In terms of the overall sequence of change in the transformation process, each next step is determined on the basis of its benefits after the success of the previous step. There is no pre-specified sequence of change.

The principles of the emerging incrementalism emphasise organisational change, not technology change. Technology change, just like change to job design or management controls, is initiated when it is obviously and immediately appropriate. It may drive change, but it may follow. Taken together, the principles of incrementalism represent a significant shift away from the more traditional obsession with unmanageably large change projects.

The incrementalist mind-set challenges technologists' deep assumption that if organisations are sufficiently stable and predictable then, given time, grand schemes can be successfully implemented. Consequently, cherished projects, such as organisation-wide architecture, are marginalised. IT professionals continue to argue that the new approach is unnecessarily costly—it breeds systems that lack uniformity and which are difficult to integrate. But the old approach has been found wanting. The retail banks' experience in the last decade is telling. While Westpac was grappling with CS90, while ANZ was wrestling with the Hogan banking system, and while the Commonwealth Bank was struggling to integrate the State Bank of Victoria's systems, the National Australia Bank was quietly building a succession of modest-sized, effective systems which have helped make it the clear market leader. The practical efficacy of incrementalism could not be clearer.

COMPETENCIES—MANAGING THE RESOURCES FOR CHANGE

Where the Fujitsu Centre's research has concentrated on eliciting practical principles for guiding the process of IT-based transformation, Professors V. Sambamurthy and R. Zmud at Florida State University have developed complementary research which focuses on what they call the IT management competencies an organisation needs. They have identified a number of IT management competencies which they have found affect business performance (see Figure 10.2). Organisations that possess these are more successful at gaining new value from IT than those that do not. Sambamurthy and Zmud therefore recommend that organisations audit their IT management competencies and work to develop those in which they are weakest.[3]

Figure 10.2 Sambamurthy and Zmud's IT change competencies

Business deployment

- examination of the potential business value of new, emerging IT;
- utilisation of multi-disciplinary teams throughout the organisation;
- effective working relationships among line managers and IT staff;
- technology transfer of successful IT applications, platforms and services;
- adequacy of IT-related knowledge throughout the organisation;
- visualising the value of IT investments throughout the organisation.

External networks

- collaborative alliances with external partners (vendors, systems integrators, competitors) to develop IT-based products and processes.

Line technology leadership

- line managers' ownership of IT projects;
- propensity of employees throughout the organisation to serve as project champions.

Process adaptiveness

- propensity of all employees to learn about and explore IT tools and applications;
- restructuring of business processes throughout the organisation;
- visualising organisational activities throughout the organisation.

IT planning

- integration of business strategic planning and IT strategic planning;
- clarity of vision regarding how IT contributes to business value;
- effectiveness of project management practices.

IT infrastructure

- restructuring of IT work processes where appropriate;
- effectiveness of software development practices.

A particularly important finding of this research is that most of the critical competencies are business-based rather than IT-based. Because much of the necessary change is organisational in character, most of the essential competencies must lie in the business functions. This highlights the fact that the changes necessary for successful IT-based transformation cannot be confined within the IT function and cannot be delegated solely to IT. It reinforces principle 7 that IT decision-making must be embedded in business decision-making.

The competencies approach, like the incrementalist approach, de-emphasises the strategic design focus of the traditional mind-set. It emphasises firms' need for an appropriate complex of people, skills, processes, knowledge, strategies and technologies. It complements the incrementalist approach in that at least half of the competencies it recommends, be developed are for managing change rather than current business performance (see Figure 10.2).

COMPLEMENTARITY OF INCREMENTALISM AND COMPETENCIES APPROACHES

Since competencies are required for change but are only acquired through the practice of change, it is easy to be deceived into thinking that incrementalism and competencies are chicken and egg, with no way of deciding which should come first. In fact, they are complements that reinforce each other. An organisation cannot expect to successfully manage IT-based change without appropriate competencies yet it cannot buy them in mature form off the shelf because they are a product of combinations of people, technology and organisation. Practical application of the incrementalist principles of change does not require a full set of mature IT change competencies. Rather, the principles help companies bootstrap their development of the IT change competencies.

CONCLUSION

While the traditional mind-set has often inhibited the achievement of satisfactory business returns on IT investments in the past, emerging approaches promise better results in the future. Although incrementalism emphasises what actions managers need to take and the competencies approach emphasises what resources are required, the two approaches are similar in rejecting the past obsession with strategic vision. They are complementary in their focus on what is needed to achieve a successful change process.

The new approaches challenge the IT industry because competencies are not products which it can supply shrink-wrapped, and IT professionals have yet to acquire the change management competencies the new approaches require. However, the principles of incrementalism appeal to business managers because they focus on practical business benefit and embody principles of prudential management. The combination of prudence and the evidence of successful practice is a powerful reason for trying the new approaches.

FURTHER READING

C. Sauer, P.W. Yetton, and associates, *Steps to the Future: Fresh Thinking on the Management of IT-Based Organizational Transformation*, Jossey-Bass, San Francisco, 1997.
This book combines recent research that shares certain assumptions about our understanding of technology and organisation. In particular, there is an emphasis on a view that sees technology and organisation as non-deterministic, with much that is important embedded in the human expertise of individuals and in the structures, process, techniques and routines of the organisation. Incrementalism is also discussed, particularly in Chapters 1, 2, 7 and 8.

The Flower and Samios case is described and analysed in more detail in P. Yetton, K.D. Johnston, and J. Craig, 'Computer-aided Architects: A Case Study of IT and strategic change', *Sloan Management Review*, 35, 4, Summer, 1994, pp. 57–67.

The Roads and Traffic Authority case is described and analysed in more detail in C. Sauer, 'Changing The Old Order: Sequencing Organisational and IT Change to Achieve Successful Organisational Transformation' in M. Khosrowpour and J. Liebowitz (eds), *Cases in Information Technology Management in Modern Organizations*, Idea Publishing, Harrisburg, 1997.

Readers can find more information on IT management competencies from Chapter 6 of *Steps to the Future: Fresh Thinking on the Management of*

IT-Based Organizational Transformation or from V. Sambamurthy, and R.W. Zmud, *IT Management Competency Assessment: A Tool for Creating Business Value Through IT*, Financial Executives Research Foundation, Morristown, NJ, 1994. This latter report also provides information about how to benchmark your own company against an international database. These ideas are discussed further in R. Agarwal, J. Ross and V. Sambamurthy, 'Sustaining Innovations Through IT-Competent Organizations: Insights from Practice' in T.J. Larsen, L. Levine and J.I. DeGross (eds), *Information Systems: Current Issues and Future Changes*, IFIP, Laxenburg, Austria, 1999. An alternative account of the necessary capabilities of the IT function can be found in D.F. Feeny and L.P. Willcocks, 'Core IS Capabilities for Exploiting Information Technology', *Sloan Management Review*, 30, 3, Spring, 1998, pp. 9–21.

11

Strategic management of value-creating networks

MICHAEL O'KEEFFE AND DAVID WILSON

Traditionally, firms have competed at the firm level in a head-to-head battle for market position. Suppliers and channel members were treated in an adversarial manner as the relationship between firms is viewed as a win-lose situation. However, for many firms, the future will be characterised by a shift from individual-level competition to competition between networks or value chains.

The value chain is the group of firms that combine to deliver a value product or service. The move from an adversarial relationship within the value chain is predicted upon the assumption that cooperative relationships yield a more effective and efficient system for delivery value to the ultimate customer.

Terms such as value chain, value-creating network and supply chain management (SCM) reflect the evolution in competition from firm versus firm to systems of firms versus other systems of firms. For example, Franklins and its value-creation network competes against the systems built by Coles and Woolworths, or the Australian pear grower packing shed and exporter system competing against the South African Outspan system.

Hence, one of the key elements of SCM is the notion of 'cooperating to compete'. As the focus of competition shifts then firms within a system can be better off by working together on cooperating. But make no mistake; competitive pressures drive the trend. In order to be an effective competitor, firms may need to be good cooperators.

Competition in the next century will be between networks of firms forcing firms to use a wider range of resources and core capabilities to be able to compete. Most firms are not able to assemble the necessary resources and core capabilities within themselves, therefore they will seek partners to provide resources and core capabilities to help them compete. This network of firms working with each other to create value for a customer is our topic for this chapter. We will describe the basic elements necessary to produce a value-creating network. The chapter concludes with a discussion of the strategic implications of value-creating network competition.

Slywotzky[1] links market value creation to the firm's business design. The business design 'is the totality of how a company selects its customers, defines and differentiates its offerings, defines the task it will perform itself and those it will outsource, goes to market, creates utility for customers, and captures profits. It is the entire system for delivery utility to customers and earning a profit from that activity'.[2] Business designs can be viewed at the firm level or within the context of a value-creating network or value chain. To understand value chains we need to understand value and its creation through combining the core capabilities of several firms. Purposeful value chain design involves the application of the business design concept to the creation of a network of firms that combine their core capabilities to create and deliver value to the ultimate consumer. Individual firms within the network can create superior business designs that provide value to their customers. The creation of firm value is linked directly to the core capabilities of individual firms. The creation of network value is linked to the combining of capabilities of the key firms in the network. To understand value chains or value-creating networks we need to understand what is value, core capabilities and the linking of firms into a network through relationships between the firms. We discuss value and then link it to core capabilities and then discuss how relationships effect the efficiency and effectiveness of a value chain. Value chains are explored and examples are provided to illustrate the concept. We conclude with a discussion of the strategic implications.

VALUE

Value is one of the most misused words in business. We use the term value to describe the relationship between the total market offering of the firm and the price of that offering. To understand customer value, we need to go back and revisit the marketing concept. The marketing concept states that customer needs drive the creation of products and services that satisfy these needs at a profit to the firm. Unfortunately, firms have not been very successful in fully implementing the marketing concept because superior technology and products would win in the marketplace. Technology and product-driven companies succeed in the marketplace with good organisation and modest marketing effort. These firms strongly believe that technology and good products are the way to win in the marketplace. However, there is a strong trend emerging to add—not replace, but *add*—the strength of marketing to the already strong product and technology base of companies as great products and technology are no longer enough to win in the complex world of the 1990s. A lot of the leading business-to-business firms have programs in place to upgrade the marketing skills of their marketers.

However, satisfying customer needs or creating a satisfied customer is no longer enough to win their loyalty. We must create better value than our competitors. Value results from the core capabilities of the firm and its partners to deliver a product that fully satisfies customer needs at a competitive price.

The market offering of the firm encompasses the technology supporting the product or service, the physical attributes of the product, the company reputation and the attributes delivered by the people representing the organisation. The customer weighs the complex bundle of attributes or market offering against competitive market offerings, with relative price being the item that relates the two market offerings. Value is the relationship of the firm's market offering to the price for the market offering. The consumer weighs the competing market offerings against their prices and determines the relative value of each offering

Value is a relative concept in that the consumer evaluates the products or services that fall into their evoked set. Comparing the value of a Timex watch to a Rolex watch is not relevant, as most purchasers of one or the other product would not see them as being equivalent choices. The buyer determines the relevant set of products or services to be considered. The consumer/customer sets the value.

When the economy was down, firms moved to convince the consumers that they delivered more value than their competitors. In many instances, it was more of the product at a given price, hence, McDonalds' development of 'value meals' which were a package bundling together a hamburger, French fries and a soft drink at a lower price than the sum of the individual items.

Value creation is more complex in business markets as we have multiple buying influences that are concerned with subsets of attributes rather than the total attribute package. A full discussion of how to measure and combine attributes is not within the bounds of this chapter. For our purposes, it is enough that the firm who can deliver value in the marketplace will win the battle for the consumer or customer.

Consumers ultimately define what is value. Most firms are in derived demand sectors of the economy in that they do not sell anything until the consumer buys a product and the effects of that sale ripple back up the value chain. The consumers for many products are firms. Personal computers, pens, fuel and other items are consumed in the operation of the business and they are not linked directly to the satisfying of consumer needs. The consumers in this case are the business firms.

CORE CAPABILITIES

Creation of value depends on the ability to deliver high performance on the attributes that are important to the customer. Competency in technology and business processes gives the firm the ability to deliver performance on important attributes. These competencies are the core competencies or core capabilities of the firm. These core competencies are rare within most firms. A single firm is fortunate if it has three or four major core competencies. To be a core competency the skill must add significant value to the market offering, it must assist the firm to access multiple markets and it must be performed at a superior level that very few firms can emulate. Core capabilities have a process and human content beyond what seems to be inherent in the Prahalad and Hamel[3] view of core competencies. For example, processes such as the ability of a Wal-Mart to manage customer information, logistical systems and electronic data systems in a way that very few firms can match gives Wal-Mart a competitive advantage in managing a large complex set of stores. 3M's ability to generate product innovations allows them to set and reach a goal of 30 per cent of current income coming from products introduced in the past few years.

Core capabilities are few and yet are the key to delivering superior value. In an industry such as the automotive industry, the technological environment has become so complex it has become very difficult for any one automotive firm to keep up with all of the core capabilities necessary to build a car. For example, the computing power now resident within a large automobile is said to be at a level in MIPS equivalent to the old IBM 360 computer. The electronic technology is only one example of the many technology changes in the automotive industry that drives them to change how they deal with suppliers.

The Ford Motor Company at one time with their Rough River Plant was perhaps one of the most integrative operations in the world. Iron ore came in one end of the complex and went out as an automobile at the other end of the complex. The Ford Motor Company was fully integrated from iron ore to weaving the materials for the seat coverings to assembly and building the total automobile. Today, the complexity of the technologies necessary to build a modern automobile has forced the automotive firms to de-integrate their operations. Underlying that also is the economics of the supplier base working with non-union labour which provides a much lower cost of operation. Nevertheless, today automotive firms combine their core capabilities of design, assembly, selling and their ability to combine with parts firms into a value-creating network for building an automobile. The need to create value has caused the automotive companies to de-integrate their operations and build strong partnering relationships with suppliers who use their core capabilities to do such key tasks as delivering electronics to the automotive producer or paint the cars. These tasks require the partners to work closely together. This need for deep relationships takes us to the third dimension, which is building partnerships and relationships.

Value chains management

The drive to create value requires the assembling of core capabilities beyond the capabilities resident within the firm. Putting together a network of firms to build the set of capabilities necessary to build a market offering that delivers high value to the customer becomes a major strategic thrust of the firm. One of the main ways that firms assemble this network of firms is through developing strong relationships with key partners who can add value to the market offering. Relationships can range from transactional relationships, where the buying firm negotiates with a set of potential suppliers for annual contracts, to deep relationships where firms integrate their activities and the supplier may have a number of employees working continuously on-site at the buyer's firm. The type of relationship can affect the efficiency of the value chain.

The logic of the marketplace is now starting to emerge. First, firms must be able to create value, but this value creation depends upon their core capabilities which in turn are limited because of the range of technologies needed to produce a product and the complexity of today's business environment. To add value-creation ability, firms must find partners and be able to manage these partnerships so that each partner profits from being within the partnership.

Adding one more layer of complexity, we argue that firms are moving into an environment in which they will not compete against each other but will become a member of a network of firms that will compete against another network of firms. We call these sets of firms value-creating networks as they have been assembled for the purpose of creating value for the customer. The original focus

Table 11.1 From transactions to relationships

	Consumer transaction	**Buyer–seller relationship**	**Value-chain partnership**
Relative position	Independent	Negotiation position/power	Interdependence
Rationale	Product/service choice	Supplier choice	Investment in the relationship
Marketing task	The 4Ps of the marketing mix	Winning the order	Developing the relationship
Measured by	Customer satisfaction	Satisfaction	Commitment to the relationship

was at the firm level. Gaining and sustaining competitive advantage depended upon understanding both the firm's value chain and how well the firm fitted into the overall value system. Sincc the mid-1980s, many firms have moved from an adversarial model of buyer–seller relationships to one of cooperation

In North America, firms are now trying to analyse and determine their position within value chains or value networks. Value-creating networks or value chains have multiple names describing the same phenomena; for example, some writers describe them as supply chains, others describe them as market networks, and others call them value chains, value nets or value-creating networks. It is a dynamic situation, as firms try to understand their position in a global business environment and understand how they fit into networks. In the next section, we will present some basic concepts on defining value chains and show examples of how they are applied.

VALUE-CREATING NETWORKS

In value-creating networks there is a fundamental transformation in the relationship between channel participants from buyer–seller choice to mutual investments in each other's business. As Table 11.1 shows, it is more useful to think in investment-related terms, rather than a buyer–seller choice framework.

In other words, rather than ask, 'do we want this company as a supplier/customer?' the question escalates to 'are we prepared to invest in this other firm?'. Even though the investment is not likely

Figure 11.1 Critical elements of creating a cooperative value chain

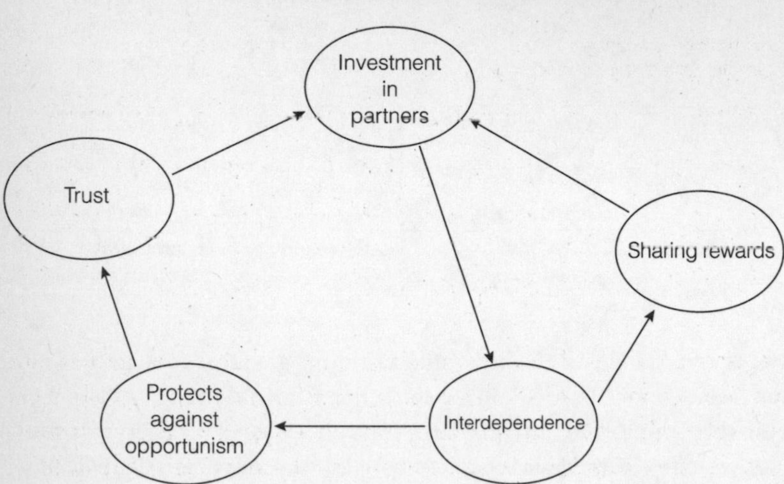

to lead to an actual ownership position, the end result is the same—a strategic commitment to the performance of the other firms in the supply chain.

The secret for successful value chains is that, as the level of investment increases, and firms consequently lose some independence, a position of mutual dependence or interdependence is created. Interdependence is what makes value chains work. The quest is not for power, but for interdependence.

The challenge in putting value networks into practice, therefore, is:

- trust-based interactions create a willingness . . .
- to make strategic investments in other value-chain firms in order . . .
- to create a position of interdependence and at the same time . . .
- to protect against opportunism and . . .
- to develop systems to share the rewards fairly . . .
- encouraging further mutual investments.

The various dimensions of value-chain networks are outlined in Figure 11.1.

By asking the question 'Are we prepared to invest in (the

Figure 11.2 The natural value chain or network

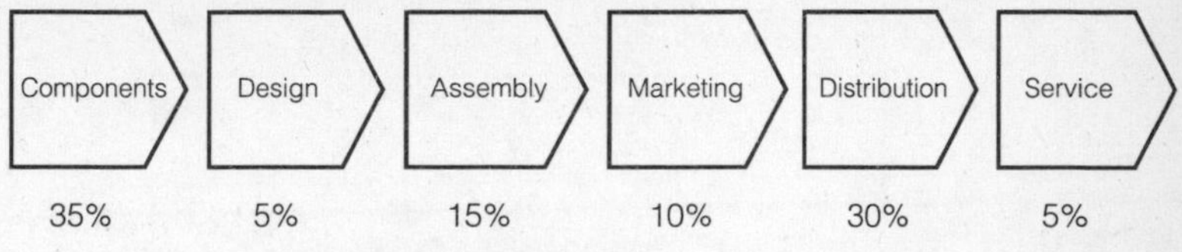

relationship with) the other business and to create a position of interdependence?' the key partnership trade-offs are highlighted. Investments are not guaranteed, but involve risk. For example, closer relationships involve a shift from 'market-risk' to 'relationship-risk'. Investments can be in people, time, or capital resources, and involve some level of risk as well as expectations of future profit.

If your firm does not impact the key attributes of the product or service then you are not in a position to extract a large share of the profits. It is critical to know your current position in the network and to devise strategies to improve your future position in the network. All business firms are part of a value-creating network. Some firms play important roles and have influence in shaping the network, while other firms play minor roles and are shaped by the network. Development of effective strategy requires understanding the firm's position within the set of networks that defines its markets and competitors. Gaining the understanding of the firm's network position requires significant effort, as we normally do not conceptualise markets and competitors in value-network terms. Traditional analysis is based upon market structures and competitors. In this section, we will describe some basic concepts of value-network analysis and then describe some examples of how these value-creating networks can be put together.

The first step in describing a value network is to describe the natural value chain or network that exists when there are no barriers between activities in the network. A natural value network is described in Figure 11.2.

This example of a natural network describes the basic steps in

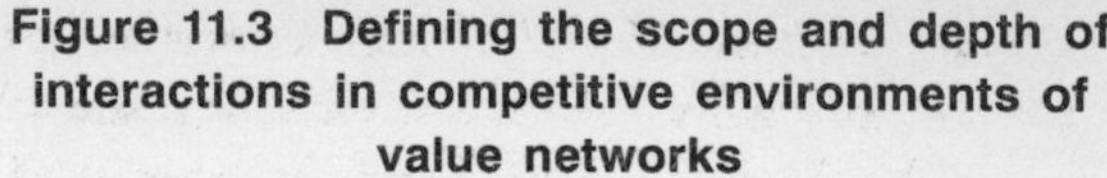

Figure 11.3 Defining the scope and depth of interactions in competitive environments of value networks

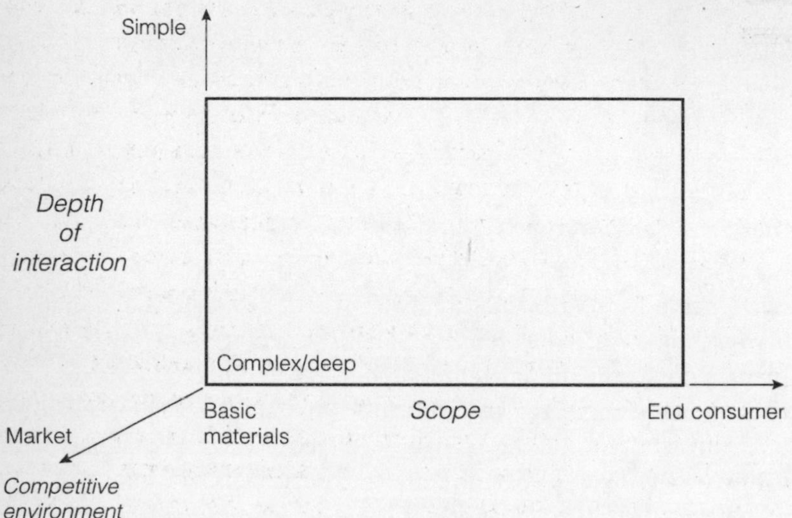

creating a computer. Obviously, the reality is far more complex, but it does give us a sense of what has to be done to create the computer. The second step is to create the enacted value network. An enacted value network represents the reality of the situation where there are barriers to the exchange of the elements of the value network which have been put in place because we are buying and selling the components. For example, if one assumes an adversarial relationship, you have a very different structure of a value network than if one assumes a cooperative set of relationships in the value network. The barriers to transaction are quite different and the cost structures are likely to be very different also. The enacted value network defines the reality of the business situation.

Figure 11.3 describes the scope, depth and competitive environment, which are dimensions that we can use to analyse value networks. The scope of the value network defines the range over which we study the value network from basic new materials to final consumer. For example, we can go back to the very basics of copper and plastics forming a circuit board, which goes into a computer, or we can assume we start at a printed circuit board level and analyse the value network forward to the retail store selling computers. As stated earlier, Ford Automotive at one time was so fully integrated that the value network began with mining iron ore from the Ford mines that was transported on Ford ships to the Ford Rough River Automotive Plant where the iron ore was converted to a Ford automobile. The range of the activities defines the scope of the value chain. A value chain could start with a printed circuit board and end with a consumer product or it could start with copper extraction and chemical manufacturing of plastic and trace the multiple steps to reach the final consumer product.

Depth of analysis describes granularity of our analysis of the activities within the value network. In the depth dimension, we only look at basic activities of assembly rather than the entire myriad of steps that goes into the assembly process. As we gain depth of analysis, we would experience greater complexity as we describe in detail the multiple activities required to create a product. Taking this fine-grained analysis for each of the multiple steps across the scope of a value chain adds more complexity.

The third dimension is studying competitive value chains to understand how we compare ourselves to competitors in terms of value created, where the value is created, who is adding to the value and the cost of value creation. The output of a value network analysis is an increased understanding of a model of how the business relates to its competitive environment. Value network analysis can define the firm's position within the network and suggest strategies to improve the position and expose where weaknesses lay and how to perhaps overcome these weaknesses.

Doing a value-network analysis challenges the firm and its model of doing business. We all have a theory of the market and how it operates and a value-network analysis provides new insights and challenges to our current model. Figures 11.4 and 11.5 provide a simple value-network analysis of two leading computer firms, Compaq and Dell. Both are exceedingly successful firms, but both have very different models of going to market. Compaq's model emerges from its early focus on being a fully compatible IBM clone. Compaq moved well beyond being a maker of clones as it set standards in the development of computers and established its own brand. Compaq relied heavily on a dealer network and have

Figure 11.4 Building toward an enacted value chain: Compaq

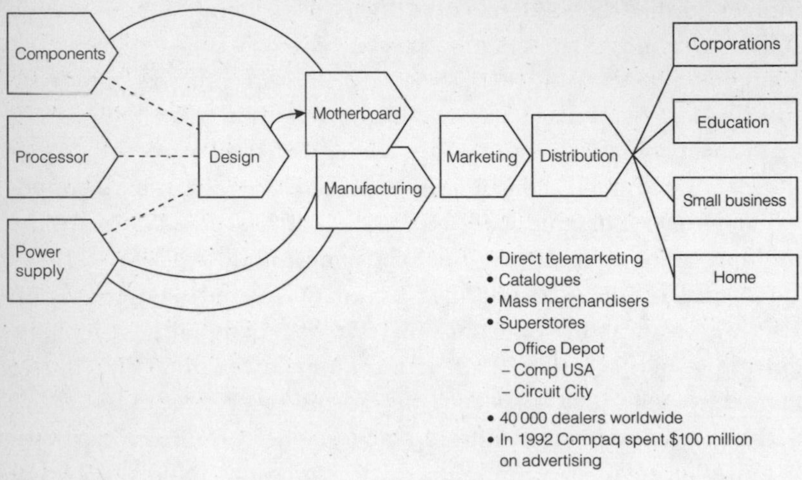

Figure 11.5 Building toward an enacted value chain: The Dell Corporation

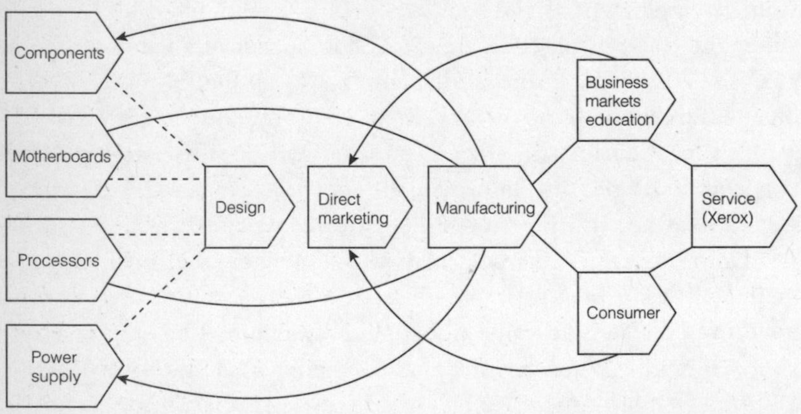

followed that model consistently throughout their emergence as a major player in the computer business. The competitive pressures from the Dell business design have caused Compaq to adjust their model to sell more directly to the consumer.

Dell's model emerges from Michael Dell's vision of the direct selling of computers. With one deviation, they have continued to follow that model. The major difference between the two models relates to when one gets paid for their product. The Dell model sells many computers where they receive payment before the computers are built, whereas the Compaq model builds computers to be held in inventory within the channels of distribution. Given the rapid technology change in the computer industry, the Compaq model carries some risk of inventory obsolescence as prices of components fall and thereby potentially lower the price of computers in inventory. The success of building the computer closer to the market has forced competitors, such as IBM, Compaq and Packard Bell to modify their business model to try to build computers closer to their customer, reducing the inventory carrying risk.

Another example of how a firm can combine core capabilities to fully exploit opportunities in the market is the development of a US firm called Calyx and Corolla. Figure 11.6 describes the traditional value network in delivering flowers to florists and consumers, while Figure 11.7 describes the Calyx and Corolla value network. The entrepreneur, Ruth Owades, saw an opportunity to sell flowers through a catalogue. She had the core capabilities of catalogue list management and catalogue creation but needed partners to develop her concept. She approached a number of growers who were wholesalers of flowers but did not sell anything at retail. She taught her partners how to package the flowers so they arrive at the customer looking like the flowers described in the catalogue. This became a core capability of the growers.

Delivering flowers on time to the customer is an important part of the concept. Ruth Owades approached Federal Express, who has a strong reputation for reliability in delivering packages to customers, to be Calyx and Corolla's delivery system. Convincing Federal Express was not an easy task because the growers are generally located in rural areas, not in high-density areas. However, when Ruth Owades approached Federal Express they were looking for new ways to grow their business and were willing to become a partner in her enterprise. Their core capability of moving things overnight and delivering them the next day was an essential ingredient in speeding the flowers to the customer. The concept was predicated upon the belief that a significant proportion of the

Figure 11.6 Distribution from grower to consumer: traditional method

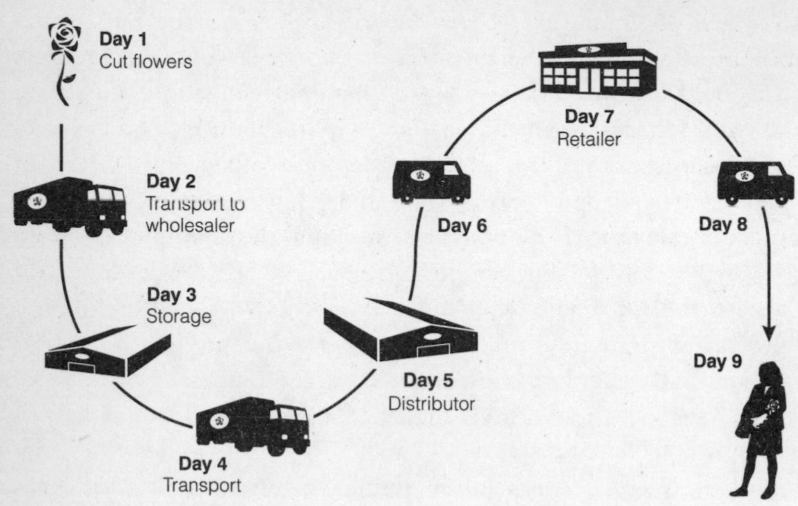

Figure 11.7 Distribution from grower to consumer: Calyx and Corolla

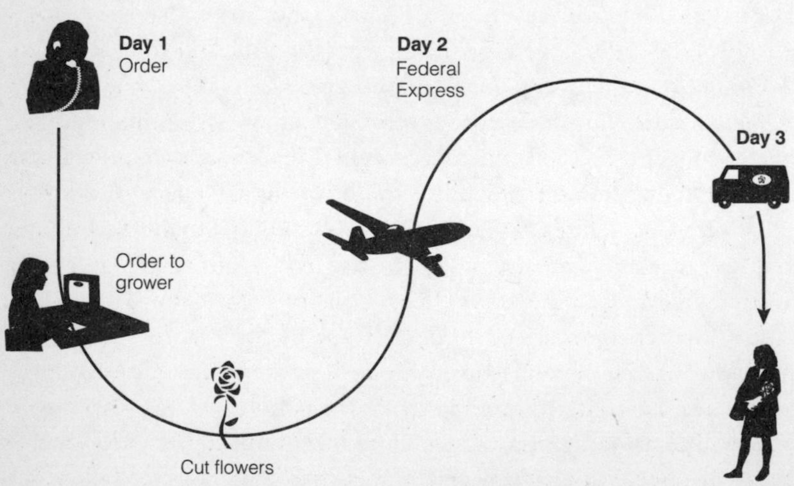

market would find value in having flowers several days fresher than they could obtain through local florists. Calyx and Corolla has been successful in developing and selling their product.

Individual trends of value creation, core capability development and the movement to a cooperative partnering environment in many firms is taking us into an era where competition is going to be defined by networks of firms rather than at the individual level. In North America, we are finding that more and more firms are beginning to develop value network or value-chain analysis as a critical step in their strategic positioning. It is in its infancy, as we cannot even agree upon a language that describes the process. It is going to be a major push in the next few years.

ELECTRONIC COMMERCE

Strategy is not simply playing the current game better, it is all about preparing to define and play the next game. Electronic commerce will be the future game for most businesses. As value networks or value chains emerge, one of the great forces shaping them is electronic commerce (e-commerce). The Dell Corporation is now selling $14 million a day or over a billion dollars a year of computers over the Internet. The cost of Internet sales is significantly lower than the cost of sales that are made through either the direct sales force calling on large organisations or through individuals talking to other individuals on the telephone. The ultimate force in redefining value networks or value chains will be e-commerce which has the potential to redefine marketplaces. The benefits of e-commerce are many, beginning with the ability to broaden the reach of the firm and offer a larger potential customer base. Geographic boundaries no longer exist and the e-commerce site, depending upon the software and hardware behind the Web site, can operate 24 hours a day, 365 days per year.

The Internet opens a new channel to service current customers and build sales with new customers. Business-to-business marketers should be natural users of e-commerce as they have a customer base that have computers and are most likely connected to the Internet. Payment systems and delivery systems are in place and management control can be established through control of who is authorised to buy and where the product may be shipped.

Electronic commerce makes it possible to reduce the costs associated with holding large physical inventories as the time gained in order processing reduces the need for holding inventories in branch locations. The value network can be connected electronically, improving the responsiveness of the system and reducing inventory.

The costs of serving a customer who specifies their needs and places an order over the Internet is significantly less than a sales call or telephone sales system. Faster customer response is accomplished with 24-hour access. Customers with questions are able to directly access centrally maintained current information. A customer can see the status of their orders and shipment information. It is possible to have a 'hot' button that will connect the customer to a 24-hour sales operation.

In some circumstances, new products can be developed working with lead users over the Internet as they respond to prototypes. Launching a new or revised product is fast because the product, specifications and price can be quickly added to the Web server and made available to the customer base.

Customer relationships exist at a different level than traditional relationships. Since e-commerce may offer the buyer a choice of how they connect with the company, either through a salesperson, over the Internet or a combination of both, each customer will be able to build the type of relationship that they prefer. A customer visit and need profile can be developed for each customer by running a data collection program in the background. This data can be used as input to new product development, target marketing and gaining better understanding of the customer.

The Internet delivers images, text and voice on hyperlinked HTML pages. Interesting multimedia presentations can make the shopping experience an educational and compelling buying experience.

Electronic commerce will not replace traditional business-to-business relationships but will become an important extension as to how business is conducted. Electronic commerce will be a potent force in redefining value networks. Channel members, such as distributors, may be the firms most at risk as their functions may be eroded as firms go direct to their customers. The term 'dis-intermediated' was coined to explain the removal of middlemen in today's world of e-commerce. The Dell Corporation is an example of a firm who chose to bypass channels of distribution and go direct to their markets. Dell is precluded from consumer markets that require a salesperson to help the customer understand their needs and options. However, once the consumer becomes knowledgeable about computers then Dell becomes a potential supplier. Within the computer market, alternative value networks compete for customers.

Strategic implications

There is a lot of uncertainty in the environment as we enter the new century. We do not know the rate at which network competition will develop. We do not know the rate at which the Web and electronic data interchange (EDI) linking between partners will develop. These are a great many unknowns, but we do know some things that are important. We know that competition will move from being competition between firms to competition between networks of firms. We know that the Web and electronic interchange and all of the products of computers and Web-based interaction will have a significant impact upon the firm in the next century. Although we do not know just how all of these changes will come about, we do know they will happen. Therefore, we need to begin to prepare ourselves to take advantage of the opportunities they create for us.

We know that value will continue to be the driver of customer choice. We know that we do not have all of the resources that our firms will need. And, we know that we will have to be involved in value-creating networks. To get ready to deal with these changes, we need to begin by understanding customer value. Utilising customer value begins by market selection. We need to understand what value is to large and important customer groups. To determine customer value requires a research program that explores groups of customers and how these needs are translated into value dimensions within the marketplace. There are two ways one can create value: (1) through the market offering of the physical product; and (2) through the exchange process. We have found in research that both of these activities contribute value to the customer. The physical product provides a great deal of the value in the exchange process but for many companies there is very little to choose between their market offering and that of the competitors. However, how the physical product and market offering is executed and exchanged provides a way to differentiate the firm on another value dimension. All firms want hassle-free partners.

Understanding customer value permits us then to make selections between markets and feed input into our product development and adjustment process. Value also determines the resources we need to be able to create the necessary value to win the marketplace battle. This in turn will lead to selection of partners on the basis of the resources and core capabilities they can bring to the value-creating network. It is the design of this network that becomes the senior manager's task. To be able to build a value-creating network requires a cultural shift within firms. One cannot take a firm that has a strong competitive drive and believes it is best to operate opportunistically with suppliers and partners and convert it overnight into a firm that believes that more value can be created by acting in a cooperative manner. The process of creating a culture and a reward structure that encourages the alignment of the many units within a firm that are necessary for successful partnerships is an important task of senior managers. If the manager does not show a strong belief in cooperation as a paradigm, then the rest of the organisation will act in an opportunistic way and destroy relationships.

Another important step in getting ready for value-creating networks is to take stock of our own value chain or value-creating network. Many firms have yet to do this basic study. Firms can describe their relations one step up and one step down the value chain. They really understand their suppliers and their first-level customer. Unfortunately, many firms do not know what happens to their product once it passes beyond their first-level customer and what are the implications of it in the marketplace. Many business firms, and particularly business-to-business firms, are in a drive demand business that is only responsive to consumer spending. We must understand what value is at the consumer level and more importantly how we contribute to that value. If we do not make a significant contribution, then we have some real problems in extracting extra value within the value-creating network.

The first step in understanding the value-creating network is to begin to incorporate value-chain analysis as part of the annual planning process. One has to expect that this will take a couple of years to fully reach its optimal point. It begins by asking each planning unit to develop a value-chain analysis for their most important markets. Reaching a full understanding may take up to two years because there is a great deal of analytical work to do. The beginning point is to understand where value is created in the chain and who contributes to its creation. The firm needs to know its role in value creation so that it can understand how to improve or consolidate their position. An important point is that the firm needs to begin now in building the skills needed for value-chain analysis.

Once the value chain is defined, it may become obvious how Internet technology may alter this value chain. It may also help to define how to use EDI and Internet technology to create additional value for participants within the chain by reducing costs of transactions and making transactions easier. There is no doubt that how we do business today and the value chains that now exist will not be the same as we enter the early years of the 21st century. Leaders in firms need to find non-competing partners to form a Web consortium to try to understand how the Web is affecting different businesses. This is an area that there are few books about and those that exist are rapidly dated. It is important that managers invest in this area and become knowledgeable so they can assess the options available to them.

The maps that guided competition when we competed against another firm like ourselves are no longer valid. We have gone beyond the edge of the map and are now looking at new territories. We seek new ways to compete as groups of firms and new technology that strengthens the groups. It is an exciting time, but a challenging one.

FURTHER READING

Up until the late 1980s the business strategy literature tended to assume that the two mechanisms for coordinating the value chain were by markets or vertical integration. Firms were considered to have discrete boundaries, and inter-firm relations were neglected. This rise of strategic alliances—the middle ground between markets and integration—changed all this. This body of literature is one of the important academic foundations of value-creating networks. A list of recommended reading follows.

Two seminal articles are those by Thorelli and Jarillo and excellent readable books for practioners have been written by Jarillo and Kay.

The *Strategic Management Journal* provides the best source of articles on linking inter-firm relationships with core capability development and competitive advantage.

At about the same time, the Scandinavian based Industrial Marketing and Purchasing Group (IMP), were becoming frustrated with the traditional consumer transaction approach to marketing, and were developing a relationship approach to business marketing. Their view was that in many business buyer–seller situations—the relationship context within which the transaction takes place becomes more important than the transaction itself. Again the theme was inter-firm relationships. Useful examples from the marketing literature are articles by Heide and John, and Morgan and Hunt. The *Journal of Marketing* publishes a number of readable articles for managers interested in following the marketing perspective.

The dependent variable in business relationship marketing is commitment to the relationship, not just satisfaction. Commitment also implies a future orientation, which is what investment is all about. Ghemawat introduces the term 'strategic commitment' which is the notion that strategy is built on investments that are durable and specialised to a particular strategy. They are non-tradeable and cannot be easily redeployed elsewhere. This captures the essence of value-creating networks—specific investments to a particular value-creation chain or system.

The book *Value Migration* by Slywotzky provides a stimulating and thought provoking overview for managers.

P. Ghemawat, *Commitment: The Dynamic of Strategy*, Free Press, New York, 1991.

J.B. Heide and G. John, 'The Role of Dependence Balancing in Safeguarding Transaction—Specific Assets in Conventional Channels', *Journal of Marketing*, 52, 1998, pp. 20–35.

J.C. Jarillo, 'On Strategic Networks', *Strategic Management Journal*, 9, 1988, pp. 33–41.

J.C. Jarillo, *Strategic Networks: Creating the Borderless Organisation*, Butterworth-Heinemann, Oxford, 1993.

J. Kay, *Foundation of Corporate Success: How Business Strategies Add Value*, Oxford University Press, Oxford, 1993.

R.M. Morgan and S.D. Hunt, 'The Commitment-Trust Theory of Relationship Marketing', *Journal of Marketing*, 58, 1994, pp. 20–38.

C.K. Prahalad and G. Hamel, 'The Core Competencies of the Corporation', *Harvard Business Review*, 68, 3, 1990, pp. 79–91.

A.J. Slywotzky, *Value Migration: How to Think Several Moves Ahead of the Competition*, Harvard Business School Press, Boston, 1996.

H.B. Thorelli, 'Networks: Between Markets and Hierarchies', *Strategic Management Journal*, 7, 1986, pp. 37–51.

12

Valuation and financial strategies

TOM SMITH AND GARRY TWITE[1]

A cynic is a person who knows the price of everything and the value of nothing.

—Oscar Wilde

This chapter examines the enduring ideas that have emerged from the field of finance, that are of relevance to businesses. Principally these are the ideas from the theory of value. The central idea here is that businesses exist to create value. If a firm did not create value, beyond what shareholders could achieve on their own, there would be no reason for it to exist. In day-to-day operations, businesses are faced with many alternative courses of action. The focus of this paper is on how a business should decide which course of action it should take. Should it lease or buy the fleet of delivery vehicles? Should it build a shopping mall or professional centre on a vacant piece of land? Should it hedge foreign exchange risk or speculate on currency movements? Should it shed this division or merge with this competitor? This chapter argues that these questions involve a comparison of risky cash flows through time and should be addressed within the valuation framework—value-based management. The business should be managed in such a way as to maximise its value. If the business practises value-based management, the answer to these operational questions is straightforward—the firm should take the course of action that adds the most value. If the firm does not practice value-based management it will either be forced to change or cease to exist.

Within this framework, this chapter addresses the important questions of:

- What is value and how is it measured?
- How does a well-run business create or add value?

Our study of value and how it is measured will introduce the three basic ideas of finance—time value of money, diversification and arbitrage—extending the discussion to consider the relationship between strategy and finance.

Our study of how a well-run business creates value will examine the:

- investment,
- financing
- risk management, and
- strategic management

functions of a business. These functions involve the comparison of risky cash flows through time, where success is judged in terms of value.

WHAT IS VALUE AND HOW IS IT MEASURED?

The three enduring ideas in finance are:

1 time value of money;
2 diversification; and
3 arbitrage.

It is these ideas that form the heart of valuation (see Figure 12.1).

Figure 12.1 The three ideas of valuation

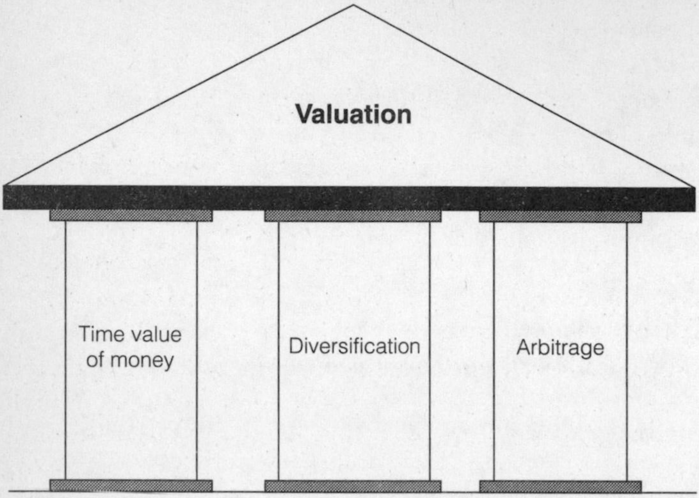

Time value of money

Historically, finance and valuation is rooted in the idea of the time value of money. The idea is centred on the work of Fisher in 1930.[2] The idea is simple—a dollar today is worth more than a dollar tomorrow. This idea is the basis of all valuation. To value any asset the approach is simple:

- write down the asset's cash flows;
- calculate the present value of the asset's cash flows; and
- sum the present values.

The value of the asset is the sum of the present values.

This approach can be used to find the value of any asset including mortgages, stocks, bonds—in fact all financing alternatives facing the firm—and investment proposals. The Net Present Value (NPV) rule indicates whether a particular investment opportunity is value adding. NPV is calculated as the difference in the present value of cash flows and investment costs. The NPV rule is the basis of other rules currently appearing in the popular press, such as Economic Value Added (EVA), Value-Based Management, Economic Profit and Cost Benefit analysis. This is not to say that there is anything wrong with these ideas. The enduring idea on which they are based, however, is the time value of money idea, as represented in the NPV rule.

Diversification

This central idea is based on the Nobel prize winning work of Markowitz[3] and Sharpe.[4] The idea here is straightforward. If investors want to make as much money as they can with least risk, they should diversify. Why? Because diversification reduces risk. The intuition here is that with a large portfolio holding, some assets will do very well, some will do very badly and most will perform up to expectations. Those that do very well will cancel out those that do very badly and fluctuations for the portfolio as a whole will be smooth and show little variation. If everyone is diversified this tells us something about how assets are priced—it gives us the required return for risk. This required return for risk is known as the Capital Asset Pricing Model (CAPM).

Because investors hold diversified portfolios, they look at each asset in terms of how it contributes to a well-diversified portfolio. Sensitivity to a well-diversified portfolio is the measure of risk (known as beta and measured relative to the market portfolio such as the All Ordinaries Index, itself a well-diversified portfolio). What return should investors require?

- For starters, they would want the return on a default-free government bond (the risk-free rate, currently around 5 per cent). This is the return they could get without taking any risk and hence they would require at least this return for investing in a risky asset.
- For every unit of risk (beta) they will demand a risk premium.
- Since risk is sensitive to the market, it seems only natural the risk premium should be that of the market. We use the market return less the risk-free rate as the measure of the market risk premium. The historical average market risk premium is 6 per cent, giving:

Required Return = Risk-Free Rate + Beta [Market Risk Premium]

It is this required return that is used in calculating present values under the time value of money idea.

Arbitrage

Modern finance began with the Nobel prize winning work of Modigliani and Miller.[5] The simple idea here is that if there are two ways to get the same cash flow they must have the same price. This idea is also known as valuation by arbitrage, 'one price only' or 'no free lunch'. Modigliani and Miller applied this idea to the firm's financing and dividend policy.

It is worth noting that this is also the idea that analysts use when they discuss the performance of your firm using price-earnings ratios and comparable firms.

The arbitrage idea is also at the heart of the valuation of futures and options. An option can be replicated by a position in the underlying stock and a bond. There are two ways of obtaining a pay-off from an option:

1 buy the option;
2 take the appropriate position in the underlying stock, financing it with a position in a bond.

Since there are two ways to get the same cash flow, the value of the option must be the known market prices of the stock and the bond. This is the basis of the Nobel prize winning work of Black and Scholes.[6]

Although the valuation of futures and options is important in its own right, the general analysis of option pricing has a much wider application. It can be applied to valuing a wide variety of corporate securities and it provides a useful analytical framework for examining a number of issues in corporate finance. For example, option pricing has been used to model the valuation of such instruments as equity, junior and senior debt, convertible notes, callable debt, rights, insurance, leases and underwriting contracts.[7] It has also been used to analyse the real options embedded within the investment opportunities available to the firm. These include the flexibility of managerial responses and the existence of strategic options.

The nature of real options

Flexibility of managerial responses refers to the additional project value that is derived by the fact that management can revise operating decisions in response to market conditions. For example, when firms have choices in how they 'manage' a project:

- delay commencement;
- abandonment;
- open/close;
- vary production; and
- selecting inputs or technologies for processing inputs.

Strategic options follow from the interdependence between existing projects and future investment opportunities. Most positive net present value projects are generated from existing projects. Strategic options include those discussed below.

- *The option to wait before investing.* For example, suppose a firm installing a power plant can delay installation for one or more years. Even if the project's NPV is positive today it still may be better to wait to invest, if by waiting we gain greater value.
- *The option to make follow-on investments* if the immediate investment project succeeds. For example, a firm may undertake investment in a research and development program for a new personal computer. If successful, it will lead initially to market testing and then to full-scale commercial production. The decision to produce at a commercial scale is a standard capital budgeting problem. The decision to invest in the research and development program is like purchasing a call option for market testing, and investing in market testing is like purchasing a call option to produce on a commercial scale.
- *The option to abandon* the investment project.

Collectively, these opportunities are called *real options*. When are these options likely to be valuable? Real options are more valuable:

- the greater the uncertainty;
- the greater the flexibility;
- the longer the time left before the investment decision must be made; and
- the higher interest rates.

Arbitrage and strategy

Finally, the arbitrage idea is also a central concept in strategy. Can other investors or businesses replicate what the firm is doing at lower cost? If so, the firm is not adding value by pursuing the strategy.

Valuation bottom line

Two decisions management face are what projects to invest in and how these projects should be funded. This decision-making process involves the comparison of risky cash flows through time. The focus is on cash, time and risk, where success is judged in terms of value.

In valuing these risky cash flows, management utilise the concepts listed below.

- The time value of money idea:
  - the value of an asset is just the present value of its cash flows—we find the present value using the required return.
- The diversification idea:
  - the required return is given by the CAPM and is equal to the Risk-Free Rate + Beta x [Market Risk Premium].
- The arbitrage idea:
  - foreign cash flows used in our NPV analysis are based on values determined using the forward exchange rates;
  - value the embedded real options.

HOW DOES A WELL-RUN BUSINESS CREATE OR ADD VALUE

Our study of how a well-run business creates value will examine the:

- investment;
- risk management;
- financing; and
- strategic management

functions of a business.

Investment

Where does the value come from in the investment function? We saw from the valuation by arbitrage idea that the answer to this is essential. What is it that the firm does that no-one else can do? If others can replicate what you do at the same or lower cost then you are adding no long-term value. An important question is whether barriers to entry exist. If so, others are not able to replicate what you are doing. If there are no barriers to entry then a successful product or financial service will be quickly replicated by competitors and there will not be a long-run sustainable competitive advantage.

An interesting example here is in the personal computer market and the company that made zip and jaz drives. These were exceptional products and the market priced the company as if there were going to be a string of innovative ideas. Instead these were the only ideas. They were quickly replicated by competitors and hence were not capable of creating a long-term source of value. The market expected that when these products were introduced, the company already had another product fully developed waiting to be released in six months' time plus other products on the drawing board ready for release in another six months and so on.

A good local example is the non-bank home financing providers such as Aussie Home Loans. These firms gained a first mover advantage, which was quickly matched by other non-bank providers and then the banks themselves. To create a long-term sustainable advantage, these firms need to be continually launching innovative products. Aussie Home Loans is attempting to do this with its home security services.

These opportunities represent real options. How do you value these real options?

Valuation of real options

In the past, conventional discounted cash flow analysis stopped with the statement: '*Accept those projects with positive NPV and reject negative NPV projects*'. The assumptions being that positive NPV equals value creation and, conversely, negative NPV equals value destruction.

Should we reject all negative NPV projects? The answer is no! But where to from here? The next step is to ask: 'What is the source of the positive NPVs?'. That is, from where does the benefit to the firm come? Any manager facing this question should start with the market price of the asset and ask why this project is worth more to our firm than to our competitors—apply the arbitrage idea. In answering this question the manager is identifying the source of the firm's sustainable advantage as it relates to this project. This is so because a positive NPV stems from sustainable advantage. For example, one benefit of a takeover of Arnott's Biscuits by Campbell's Soups is that Campbell's Soups gains access to the distribution channel and brand name recognition of Arnott's Biscuits. The distribution channel and brand name recognition will give Campbell's Soups a valuable sustainable advantage.

Think of those activities which easily illustrate the building of sustainable advantage:

- research and development;
- exploration; and
- access to new markets.

If a project has a negative NPV, these activities may still provide a reason for investing. They may offer the company a follow-on opportunity, which is valuable. Valuing the initial investment and the follow-on investment might appear as a simple valuation problem—write down the cash flows for both investments and discount them to determine the NPV for the two investments taken together. What are we ignoring? The follow-on investment is discretionary, and whether or not it is undertaken depends upon uncertain future conditions—the outcome of the initial project. The follow-on investment is an option (see Figure 12.2[8]).

One problem in applying NPV analysis to real options is that the possible cash flows and associated probabilities are difficult and complex to specify. The financial manager must recognise the value of the options created by the initial project and not reject it simply because it is a negative NPV project by itself. The decision to undertake the project requires that management consider the NPV of both the initial project and the options it creates.

One valuation approach is to apply existing option pricing models, such as the Black-Scholes option pricing model. However, there are several problems in applying existing option pricing

Figure 12.2 Valuing opportunities is different

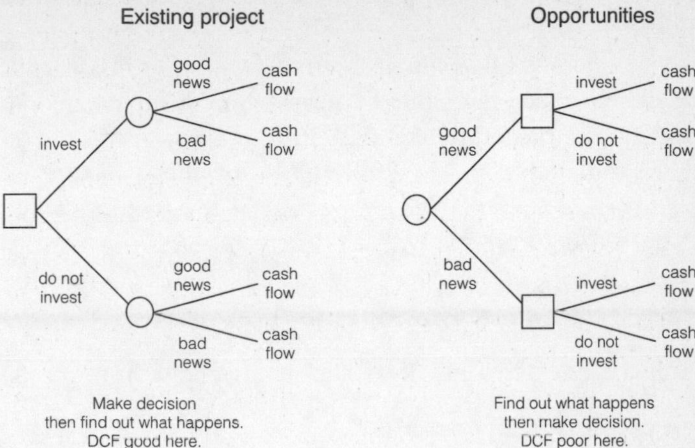

models to real options. Contrary to model requirements, the present value of the project, the required outlay and the time left before the investment decision must be made, may not be certain for the real options. The required outlay and the time left before the investment decision must be made will vary according to the actions of the firm's competitors. Real options may not be proprietary; that is, the firm may not be the only one able to exercise the option, such as the development of microcomputers.

Decision tree analysis may help to overcome the problems of both simple NPV analysis and the difficulties in applying the option pricing models to real options (an illustration of the application of decision tree analysis to real options can be found in the 1990 article by Copeland and Weiner which appeared in the *McKinsey Quarterly*).[9]

A further approach to valuing real options is the use of sensitivity analysis or simulation. The value of the asset underlying the option is varied and its impact on the value of the project or firm is determined, where the operations of the project are varied as if the firm optimally utilised managerial flexibility. The resultant range represent the value added by the embedded real options.

A cavaet

Managers must recognise that the view held under conventional discounted cash flow analysis, that higher uncertainty (risk), higher interest rates and longer investment horizons reduce the NPV of a project, does not necessarily hold once we recognise the existence of real options.

Higher uncertainty, higher interest rates and longer investment horizons may not reduce the value of an investment project. While these factors reduce the value of the existing project, they increase the value of the real options. The impact of these factors on the project value depends on the proportion of the project's value generated by real options.

Risk management

In today's global environment, firms almost invariably have a:

- foreign exchange exposure;
- interest rate exposure.

In most cases the core competency of the firm is in making and selling its product and not in foreign exchange speculation or interest rate speculation. In these circumstances, it may be appropriate to hedge the risks of foreign exchange and interest rate fluctuations. Is this something that adds value to the business? Again the valuation by arbitrage idea is of central importance. How easy is it for investors to hedge these risks themselves? If it is easy they would prefer to hedge their net exposures over their entire portfolio rather than having each individual company hedging its exposure. Some factors that may influence whether the company or the individual investors should hedge are listed below.

- *Information*. Sometimes it is not in a company's interest to publicly release its foreign exchange or interest rate exposures and hence individual investors will not be aware of these.
- *Transaction costs*. Firms should be able to transact at wholesale rates whereas individual investors will receive retail rates.
- *Taxes*. Under current tax laws gains on hedging can be offset against losses made by the firm. Since individual investors do not have an offsetting loss when they hedge, the gains on hedging are assessable.

For these reasons, it might be preferable for the firm rather than the individual to hedge. However, is it desireable to hedge at all? There may well be a valuable strategic option of which management can take advantage. An example here is foreign exports denominated in the foreign currency. If the currency moves favourably in the firm's direction, this is a windfall. If the currency moves against the firm, management may be flexible enough to get out of the contract. An abandonment option of this kind is very valuable.

Financing

The firm's financing decisions add value by providing the source of funds needed to carry out the business of the firm. But does the firm's capital structure, that is, the mix of debt and equity, affect value? For example, can a firm add value by restructuring so that it has more debt? Again the valuation by arbitrage idea is of central importance. If it is easy for individual investors to replicate the debt and equity structure of the firm there will be no value added by restructuring the debt and equity of the firm. In Australia, where we have a dividend imputation scheme, the net tax advantage of debt over equity is minimal.

However, the question remains as to whether the firm's financing and investment decisions are inter-related beyond the function of providing the necessary funds. That is, can the firm's financing decisions impact on the overall strategy of the firm?

The answer is yes! The firm's financing decisions can affect non-financial stakeholders (including employees, suppliers and customers) and they in turn influence the success of the firm's strategy (see Figure 12.3[10]). To illustrate, let us take one possible, albiet extreme, outcome of the firm's financing decisions; namely, the likelihood of the firm experiencing financial distress.

The likelihood of the firm experiencing financial distress can impact on non-financial stakeholders. Employers may lose entitlements (long service leave or superannuation) or their job; customers may receive inferior products, have warranties voided or experience difficulty in receiving service; and suppliers may lose business.

The firm's financial decisions can affect how the firm is viewed by its customers, employees, suppliers and any other firm or individual that in some way have a stake in its success. The stakeholder's views are especially important for firms whose products need future

Figure 12.3 The links between financing decisions and corporate strategy

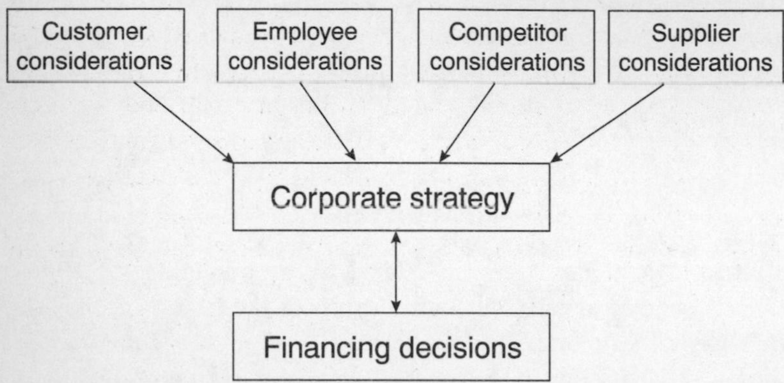

servicing (such as automobiles and computers) or whose product quality is important but difficult to observe (such as prescription drugs). Financial distress can also be costly for firms that require their employees and suppliers to invest in product-specific training and physical capital. On the other hand, firms that produce non-durable goods (such as agricultural products) or provide services that are not particularly specialised (such as hotel rooms) probably have low financial distress costs.

Because of the costs they potentially bear in the event of a firm's financial distress, non-financial stakeholders will be less interested, all else being equal, in doing business with a firm in financial difficulties. This understandable reluctance can deter a firm from making use of debt financing, even when lenders are willing to provide it on favourable terms.

The implication is that non-financial stakeholders' opinions of the firm's capital structure influences their view of the firm. This influences the opportunities available to the firm and its overall strategy.

Finally, from our discussion of real options we see that operating flexibility is an important source of sustainable advantage. How does management maintain operating flexibility? The answer is that management requires financial flexibility to maintain operating flexibility. The degree of financial flexibility required is related to the operating risk of the firm. Adverse economic events could severely damage a highly levered firm's competitive position. Moreover, the more highly levered the firm is, the more it will be subject to debt covenants. These will further constrain management's choice of operating, and financial and investment policies, and hence reduce its capacity to respond to changes in the business environment. The reduction in operating and financial flexibility will prove especially costly to firms competing in product and factor markets which are continually changing. This includes firms whose markets are undergoing deregulation and high-technology firms. In contrast, firms operating in stable markets can afford more debt because their competitive position will be less compromised by the restrictions and delays associated with high financial leverage.

Recognising this relationship between financial and operating risks, firms are likely to maintain substantial financial resources in the form of unused debt capacity, large quantities of liquid assets, excess lines of credit and access to a broad range of fund sources. Thus financial flexibility helps preserve operating flexibility.

Strategic management

Should the focus of management be on total quality management? Should the focus of management be on growth? Should the focus of management be on service to the customer, the environment or . . .? We argue that the focus of the firm should be on adding value to the business. In determining the optimal strategy one simple rule should be followed—*the best strategy is the one that adds the most value.*

Value creation bottom line

In seeking to create value, the firm should focus on the investment decision:

- valuable investment opportunities provide the firm with sustainable competitive advantage;
- sustainable competitive advantage comes from the existence of real options; and
- always maintain operating flexibility.

In deciding whether to hedge, the firm must consider:

- the nature of its core competency; and
- the extent of flexibility around risk management.

In deciding on the firm's capital structure:

- recognise the relationship between financial and operating risks;
- maintain financial flexibility as financial flexibility preserves operating flexibility; and
- don't ignore the interaction with non-financial stakeholders, as leverage affects the firm's ability to do business with non-financial stakeholders.

FURTHER READING

M. Miller, 'The Modigliani Miller Propositions After Thirty Years', *Journal of Economic Perspectives*, Fall, 1988, pp. 99–120.
While focusing on the firm's financing and dividend decisions, this is an excellent summary of where the discussion around the no-arbitrage concept has evolved.

S.C. Myers, 'Finance Theory and Financial Strategy', *Midland Corporate Finance Journal*, Spring, 1987, pp. 6–13.
This article is an excellent primer that develops the link between finance and strategy.

T.A. Luehrman, 'Strategy as a Portfolio of Real Options', *Harvard Business Review*, September–October 1998, pp. 89–99.
This article explores the link between sustainable advantage and real option, postulating that the firm's strategy is best represented as a portfolio of real options.

T.A. Luehrman, 'Investment Opportunities as Real Options: Getting Started on the Numbers', *Harvard Business Review*, July–August 1998, pp. 51–66.
This article is an excellent introduction to the valuation of real options.

L. Trigeorgis, *Real Options: Managerial Flexibility and Strategy in Resource Allocation*, MIT Press, Massachusetts, 1996.
This book provides a detailed discussion of real options, including issues around definition, identification, implications and valuation of real options.

13

The future

GARRY TWITE

Strategy is at the dawn of a new era. As academia has searched for the sources of sustainable advantage, three alternative views have evolved—the *industry view*, the *resource-based view* and the *relational view*.

All three approaches seek to identify the source of sustainable competitive advantage to the firm and would agree that it is represented by an 'asset' unique to the firm. However, they differ on the question of where this 'asset' resides. The industry-based view would argue that sustainable competitive advantage stems from both the industry structure and the firm's position within the industry, while both the resource-based and relational views would argue that sustainable competitive advantage stems from assets or resources unique to the firm, the resource-based view argues that these resources reside within the firm, while the relational view argues that they reside within the relationships that the firm has with its various stakeholders—suppliers, customers, substitutors and complementors.

Both the resource-based and relational views agree that sustainable competitive advantage is based on resources and assets that are:

- unique;
- lack a substitute;
- flexible or dynamic; and
- durable.

In common, both views would identify two resource classes that meet this requirement, and are therefore potential sources of sustainable competitive advantage; namely, IT management (including the utilisation of e-commerce) and intangibles (including corporate knowledge and reputation). However, they differ on the question of where these resources reside. The resource-based view would argue that it is the firm's utilisation of IT, its development of organisational knowledge and its corporate reputation that creates value. While the relational view argues that it is the utilsation of IT, sharing of knowledge and the reputation of the partnership that creates value.

The most likely answer to this debate is that it varies across firms. For some it is those resources that are unique to the firm that drive value creation, while for others, value creation comes from its network.

The underlying message of both the resource-based and relational views is that real options are valuable, wherever located—within the firm or as part of its network.

STRATEGY INTO THE FUTURE

What is the likely focus of business strategy into the new millennium?

While the firm will remain the focus for developing sustainable competitive advantage, it is no longer the sole focus. We now recognise that networks of allied firms are creating sustainable competitive advantage through cooperation. In order to be an effective competitor, firms may need to be good cooperators—the notion of 'cooperating to compete'.

Within this context, what are the likely candidates for sources of sustainable advantage? The importance of IT and the emergence of e-commerce suggests that IT generally, and e-commerce particularly, will be one of the forces shaping value creation in the future. The other potential source of sustainable competitive advantage in the future are intangible assets, including knowledge utilisation and reputation.

MANAGEMENT IMPLICATIONS

While we recognise that firms can create value through the possession of unique, non-replicable, firm-specific assets, cooperating firms can also create value through the building of relation-specific assets, knowledge sharing and the utilisation of complementary resources. The focus for managers must be on identifying those resources which represent the drivers of profitability. In analysing the firm's value creation potential, while focusing on assets that lie within the firm, managers must look beyond the firm's boundaries—identify the firm's value-creation chain. The task for management is to identify potential value-creating assets then build and maintain sustainable advantage.

Management must recognise that sustainable competitive advantage is built not bought. The current view states that if you can buy it—or it is tradeable—it can be replicated by others; hence, it is unlikely to lead to a sustainable competitive advantage. The implication is that core capabilities are built, not bought.

In building sustainable competitive advantage management should focus on small rather than big decisions. The process of building sustainable competitive advantage should be undertaken incrementally—building on existing competencies. Management will assess the value added by each decision. In adopting this approach we seek value increasing changes, while limiting the risk to the current step.

In seeking to establish a sustainable competitive advantage, management should look beyond the firm's boundaries; don't ignore other stakeholders—customers, suppliers, substitutors and complementors. Management shouldn't just focus on resources idiosyncratic to the firm. We must recognise that sustainable competitive advantage can arise through cooperation. The implication for management is to look to the firm's network as a source of profitability.

Having built a sustainable competitive advantage, the next step for management is to maintain that advantage.

Competitive advantage is a fragile construct, it must be maintained. The creation and defence of sustainable advantage is a dynamic process, suggestive of a process of corporate change. The key to change is flexibility, it is operating flexibility that enables the firm to change in response to changing market conditions. The implication is that management should seek to maintain flexibility.

To be effective in achieving change, management must achieve three things:

1 the *engagement* of the stakeholders in the firm—including employees, customers and suppliers;
2 the *development* of the firm's resources to meet the needs of the change; and
3 the simultaneous *management* of both the change process and the firm's ongoing operations.

How does this process translate to managing sustainable advantage developed from knowledge utilisation or corporate reputation? To maintain a sustainable advantage achieved through knowledge utilisation the firm must exhibit 'the three c's':

1 c*reativity* in its ability to solve problems;
2 *comprehensiveness* in its ability to gather, retain and synthesise information; and
3 *consensus* in its decision-making know-how.

To maintain a sustainable competitive advantage achieved via building the firm's corporate reputation, management must:

1 identify what the organisation *stands* for;
2 identify the *factors* that determine its reputation;
3 *don't* do anything likely to *destroy* the firm's reputation; and finally, and possibly most important,
4 *communicate* to both internal and external stakeholders.

The bottom line for managers is that real options are valuable wherever located. Management should look both within the firm and to the firm's network of customers, suppliers, substitutors and complementors to identify potential sources of competitive advantage. Once identified, management should seek to build sustainable advantage through a process of incremental decisions, assessing the value added at each step in the process. This created advantage should be maintained and defended—management should adapt to change—maintain flexibility.

FURTHER READING

A. Brandenburger and B. Nalebuff, 'The Right Game: Use Game Theory to Shape Strategy', *Harvard Business Review*, July–August 1995, pp. 57–71.
This article explores what is becoming an increasingly important part of strategic analysis; namely, what games theory can tell the firm about ways to structure its strategy—particularly networks and value chains. The underlying theme of the article is to look at both cooperative and competitive ways to structure the firm's strategy—what the authors call *coopetition*.

J. Dyer and H. Singh, 'The Relational View: Cooperative Strategy and Sources of Interorganizational Competitive Advantage', *Academy of Management Review*, 23, 1998, pp. 660–79.
This article offers the reader a thorough understanding of the development and relationship between the resource-based and relational views of sustainable advantage. The underlying theme is to look beyond the firm's boundaries for competitive advantage.

T.A. Luehrman, 'Strategy as a Portfolio of Real Options', *Harvard Business Review*, September–October 1998, pp. 89–99.
This article explores the link between sustainable advantage and real options—postulating that the firm's strategy is best represented as a portfolio of real options. This approach enables us to see the links between the various components of the firm's overall strategy. The key message of the article is that by building an option's framework into the decision-making process management can add financial insights into strategic analysis.

D. Teece, 'Capturing Value from Knowledge Assets', *California Management Review*, 40, 3, 1988, pp. 55–79.
This is the introductory article to a special issue of the *California Management Review* on knowledge. Look at the whole issue if you get a chance. This article seeks to explore knowledge as a key source of

competitive advantage for the firm. The key message of the article is that knowledge and other intangibles have emerged as the primary sources of competitive advantage. By implication, management must focus on the development and maintenance of intangibles.

Notes

1 INTRODUCTION

1 M. Porter, *Competitive Strategy: Techniques for Analyzing Industries and Competitors*, Free Press, New York, 1980.

2 J. Roquebert, R. Phillips and P. Westfall, 'Market vs. Management: What "Drives" Profitability?', *Strategic Management Journal*, 17, 1996, pp. 653–64.

3 A. McGahan and M. Porter, 'How Much Does Industry Matter, Really?', *Strategic Management Journal*, 18, 1997, pp. 15–30.

4 B. Wernerfelt, 'A Resource-based View of the Firm', *Strategic Management Journal*, 5, 1984, pp. 171–80.

5 A. Brandenburger and B. Nalebuff, 'The Right Game: Use Game Theory to Shape Strategy', *Harvard Business Review*, July–August 1995, pp. 57–71.

6 J. Dyer and H. Singh, 'The Relational View: Cooperative Strategy and Sources of Interorganizational Competitive Advantage', *Academy of Management Review*, 23, 1998, pp. 660–79.

7 The following table is adapted from Dyer and Singh, 1998, op. cit., p. 674.

2 COMPETITION POLICY

1 'The Committee is to inquire into and advise on appropriate changes to legislation and other measures in relation to:
(a) whether the scope of the *Trade Practices Act* 1974 should be expanded to deal with anti-competitive conduct of persons or enterprises in areas of business currently outside the scope of the Act;
(b) alternative means for addressing market behaviour and structure currently outside the scope of the *Trade Practices Act* 1974; and
(c) other matters directly related to the application of the principles above'. Independent Committee of Inquiry into Competition Policy in Australia, *National Competition Policy*, AGPS, Canberra, 1993, p. 362.

2 OECD, Regulatory Reform, Privatisation & Competition Policy, 1992, p. 43.

3 George J. Stigler, *Memoirs of an Unregulated Economist*, Basic Books, Inc., New York, 1988.

4 Joseph A. Schumpeter, quoted by George Stigler, *Memoirs of an Unregulated Economist*, Basic Books, Inc., New York, 1988, p. 101.

5 Industry Commission, 'Does Pacific Power Have Market Power?', a report on the implications for the National Electricity Market of New South Wales Generation Options, August 1995.

6 London Economics and David Harbord and Associates, 'Market Power in the Australian Electricity Market', a report to the Industry Commission, August 1995.

7 Richard J. Green and David M. Newbery, 'Competition in the British Electricity Spot Market', *Journal of Political Economy*, 100, 1992, pp. 929–52.

8 Nils Henrik Merch von der Fehr and David Harbord, 'Spot Market Competition in the UK Electricity Industry', *The Economic Journal*, May 1993, pp. 531–46.

9 One explanation for the apparent difference between the Stigler findings and the electricity results, suggested by George Hay, is that in the studies cited by Stigler the number of potential bidders were greater than the actual bidders, while in the electricity studies all potential bidders were in the market, and the models did not take adequate account of entry or potential entry.

10 See, for example, Williams W. Sharkey and David S. Sibley, 'A Bertrand Model of Pricing and Entry', *Economics Letters*, 41, 1993, pp. 199–206.

11 See, for example, Avinash K. Dixit and Robert S. Pindyck, *Investment Under Uncertainty*, Princeton University Press, Princeton, NJ, 1993.

12 See, for example, Colin F. Camerer, 'Does Strategy Research Need Game Theory?' in *Fundamental Issues in Strategy*, edited by Richard P. Rumelt, Dan E. Schendel and David J. Teece, Harvard Business School Press, Boston, 1994, pp. 195–219.

13 Stephen P. King, 'Access Pricing', Research Paper No. 3, Government Pricing Tribunal of New South Wales, February 1995.

14 ibid.

15 Avinash K. Dixit and Robert S. Pindyck, *Investment Under Uncertainty*, Princeton University Press, Princeton, NJ, 1993, p. 296.
16 H. Demsetz, 'How Many Cheers for Antitrust's 100 Years?', *Economic Inquiry*, 30, 1992, pp. 207–17.
17 *Independent Committee of Inquiry, National Competition Policy*, Australian Government Publishing Service, Canberra, August 1993, p. 245. See also George A. Hay, 'Reflections on *Clear*', *Competition and Consumer Law Journal*, 3, 1996, pp. 231–44.
18 P. Yetton, J. Craig, J. Davis and F. Hilmer, 'Are Diamonds a Country's Best Friend? A Critique of Porter's Theory of National Competition as Applied to Canada, New Zealand and Australia', *Australian Journal of Management*, 17, 1, June 1992, pp. 89–120.
19 *Economist*, 13 August 1994, p. 64.

3 BUSINESS STRATEGY AND INDUSTRY POLICY

1 D. North, *Institutions, Institutional Change and Economic Performance*, Cambridge University Press, Melbourne, 1992, p. 131.
2 J. Dunning (ed), *Governments, Globalisation and International Business*, Oxford University Press, Oxford, 1997; also, *Alliance Capitalism and Global Business*, Routledge, London, 1997.
3 ibid., p. 15.
4 D. North, 1992, op. cit.
5 Arthur Dentzau and Douglass North, 'Shared Mental Models, Ideologies and Institutions', *Kyklos*, 47, 1994, pp. 3–31.
6 For example, I. Marsh, *Beyond the Two Party System? Political Representation, Economic Competitiveness and Australian Politics*, Cambridge University Press, Melbourne, 1995.
7 M. Porter, 'Clusters and the New Economics of Competition', *Harvard Business Review*, November 1998, pp. 77–90.
8 S. Strange, *The Retreat of the State*, Cambridge University Press, Melbourne, 1996.
9 J. Dunning, *The Globalisation of Business: The Challenge of the 1990s*, Routledge, London, 1993 and K. Ohmae, *The End of the Nation State*, HarperCollins, New York, 1995.
10 For example, E. Schein, *Strategic Pragmatism: The Culture of Singapore's Economic Development Board*, MIT Press, Cambridge, 1996.

4 THE TRIUMPH OF THE FIRM

1 I should like to mention my late wife, Hazel Church, and Robin Stonecash, both of whom gave me useful comments.

2 J. Maynard Keynes, *The General Theory of Employment Interest and Money*, Macmillan for the Royal Economic Society, London, 1973, (1936), p. 383.
3 See F. Knight, 'From Risk, Uncertainty and Profit' in L. Putterman and R. Kroszner (eds), *The Economic Nature of the Firm: A Reader*, 2nd edn, Cambridge University Press, Cambridge, 1996.
4 R. Coase, *The Firm, the Market, and the Law*, Chicago University Press, Chicago, 1988.
5 See O. Williamson, 'The Limits of Firms: Incentive and Bureaucratic Features', Chapters 9 and 11 of Putterman and Kroszner, op. cit.
6 H. Demsetz, *The Economics of the Business Firm: Seven Critical Commentaries*, Cambridge University Press, Cambridge, 1995.
7 O. Hart, *Firm Contracts and Financial Structure*, Clarendon Press, Oxford, 1995.

5 KNOWLEDGE, TACIT UNDERSTANDING AND STRATEGY

1 M. Porter, *Competitive Strategy: Techniques for Analyzing Industries and Competitors*, Free Press, New York, 1980.
2 G. Hamel and C.K. Prahalad, 'The Core Competence of the Corporation', *Harvard Business Review*, 68, May/June 1990, pp. 79–87.
3 G. Stalk, P. Evans and L. Shulman, 'Competing on Capabilities', *Harvard Business Review*, 70, March/April 1992, pp. 57–69.
4 R. Coase, 'The Theory of the Firm', *Economica*, 4, 1937.
5 F. Hayek, *The Use of Knowledge in Society*, Institute for Humane Studies, Menlo Park CA, 1970.
6 J. Schumpeter, *The Theory of Economic Development*, Harvard University Press, Cambridge MA, 1934.
7 See Sun Tzu, *The Art of War*, S. Griffith (trans.), Oxford University Press, Oxford, 1963.
8 F. Dretske, *Knowledge and the Flow of Information*, MIT Press, Cambridge MA, 1981, pp. 44, 81.
9 F. Machlup, *Knowledge: Its Creation, Distribution and Economic Significance*, (two volumes), Princeton University Press, Princeton NJ, 1980.
10 W. James, *The Meaning of Truth: A Sequel to 'Pragmatism'*, Longmans, Green, London, 1910.
11 D. Teece, 'Profiting from Technological Innovation: Implications for Integration, Collaboration, Licensing and Public Policy', *Research Policy*, 15, 1986, pp. 285–305.
12 See D. Leonard-Barton, *Wellsprings of Knowledge: Building and Sustaining the Sources of Innovation*, Harvard Business School Press, Cambridge MA, 1996.

13 I. Nonaka and H. Takeuchi, *The Knowledge Creating Company*, Oxford University Press, New York, 1995.
14 A. Ginsberg, 'Minding the Competition: From Mapping to Mastery', *Strategic Management Journal*, 15, 1994, pp. 153–74.
15 *The Hitopadesa: The Book of Wholesome Counsel*, F. Johnson (trans.), Chapman and Hall, London, 1928. *The Hitopadesa* is a set of Sanskrit fables thought to have been written between 600–1100 AD.

6 CORPORATE SUPER-BRANDS

1 See, for example, K. Weigelt and C. Camerer, 'Reputation and Corporate Strategy: A Review of Recent Theory and Applications', *Strategic Management Journal*, 9, 5, pp. 443–54.
2 See, for example, D. Bernstein, *Company Image and Reality*, Cassell, London, 1984 and S. Howard, *Corporate Image Management*, Butterworth-Heinemann, Singapore, 1998.
3 See, for example, W. Olins, *Corporate Identity: Making Business Strategy Visible through Design*, Harvard Business School Press, Boston, 1989.
4 See, for example, S. Hunt and R. Morgan, 'The Comparative Advantage Theory of Competition', *Journal of Marketing*, 59, 2, 1995, pp. 1–15.
5 P. Roberts and G. Dowling, 'The Value of a Firm's Corporate Reputation: How Reputation Helps Attain and Sustain Superior Profitability', *Corporate Reputation Review*, 1, 1 and 2, 1997, pp. 72–6.
6 See, for example, R. Srivastava, T. McInish, R. Wood and A. Capraro, 'The Value of Corporate Reputation: Evidence from the Equity Markets', *Corporate Reputation Review*, 1, 1 and 2, 1997, pp. 62–8 and D. Deephouse and E. Ourso, 'The Effect of Financial and Media Reputation on Performance', *Corporate Reputation Review*, 1, 1 and 2, 1997, pp. 68–72.
7 *Fortune* magazine, 2 March 1998, pp. 38–53 and F–1 to F–7.
8 See, for example, R. Worcester, 'Corporate Image Research' in R. Worcester (ed.), *Consumer Research Handbook*, McGraw-Hill, London, 1972, S. Kennedy, 'Nurturing Corporate Images', *European Journal of Marketing*, 11, 3, 1977, pp. 120–64, E. Dichter, 'What's in an Image?', *The Journal of Consumer Marketing*, 2, 1, 1985, pp. 75–81.
9 *Fortune* magazine, op. cit.
10 See, for example, J. Rossiter and L. Percy, *Advertising Communications and Promotion Management*, McGraw-Hill, New York, 1997.
11 D. Gross, *Forbes Greatest Business Stories of All Time*, John Wiley & Sons, New York, 1996, p. 1.
12 R. Jacobson and D. Aaker, 'The Strategic Role of Product Quality', *Journal of Marketing*, 51, 4, 1987, pp. 31–44.

13 S. Kerr, 'On the Folly of Rewarding A, While Hoping for B', *Academy of Management Journal*, December 1975, pp. 769–83.

14 M. Gilly and M. Wolfinbarger, 'Advertising's Internal Audience', *Journal of Marketing*, 62, 1, 1998, pp. 69–88.

15 For some good examples of this strategy see A. Ries and J. Trout, *Positioning: The Battle for Your Mind*, McGraw-Hill, New York, 1986.

16 The impact of corporate identity on these factors is often measured here.

7 SCHUMPETER AND THE DYNAMICS OF FIRM STRATEGY

1 R. Nelson, 'Institutions Supporting Technical Advance in Industry', *American Economic Review*, 76, 1986, p. 196.

2 D. Mueller, *The Dynamics of Company Profits: An International Comparison*, Cambridge University Press, Cambridge, 1990.

3 R. Nelson and S. Winter, *An Evolutionary Theory of Economic Change*, Harvard University Press, Cambridge, 1982.

4 W. Cohen and R. Levin, 'Empirical Studies of Innovation and Market Structure' in R. Schmalansee and R. Willing (eds), *Handbook of Industrial Organization*, volume II, Elsevier Science Publishers, Amsterdam, 1989.

5 J. Schumpeter, *Capitalism, Socialism and Democracy*, Harper, New York, 1950, p. 84.

6 Schumpeter's entrepreneur is responsible for innovative new goods, new methods of production, new markets for existing products and new forms of organisation.

7 J. Schumpeter, *The Theory of Economic Development*, Harvard University Press, Cambridge, 1934, p. 68.

8 In support of this point, P. Geroski, S. Machin and J. Van Reenen ('The profitability of innovating firms', *RAND Journal of Economics*, 24, 1993, pp. 198–211) look at major innovations in a sample of 539 UK firms and find that each innovation raises the margins of innovating firms by some 16.5 per cent relative to the sample mean.

9 J. Schumpeter, 1934, op. cit., p. 89.

10 Based on this insight, current strategy frameworks recognise the general tendency for innovations to attract imitation. They also recognise that the intensity of this imitative process may vary because imitation is more difficult and/or costly for some innovations than for others (R.P. Rumelt, 'Toward a strategic theory of the firm' in R. Lamb (ed.), *Competitive Strategic Management*, Prentice-Hall, Englewood Cliffs, 1984, pp. 556–70, and 'Theory, strategy and entrepreneurship' in D. Teece (ed.), *The Competitive Challenge: Strategies for Industrial Innovation and Renewal*, Ballinger Publishing Co., Cambridge, 1987;

J.R. Williams, 'How sustainable is your competitive advantage?', *California Management Review*, Spring, 1992, pp. 29–51).

11 D. Mueller, 'The Persistence of Profits Above the Norm', *Economica*, 44, 1977, pp. 369–80.

12 P. Geroski, 'Modelling Persistent Profitability' in D. Mueller (ed.), *The Dynamics of Company Profits*, Cambridge University Press, Cambridge, 1990, p. 19.

13 J. Barney, 'Firm Resources and Sustained Competitive Advantage', *Journal of Management*, 17, 1991, pp. 99–120.

14 K. Conner, 'A Historical Comparison of Resource-based Theory and Five Schools of Thought Within Industrial Organization Economics: Do We Have a New Theory of the Firm?', *Journal of Management*, 17, 1991, pp. 121–54.

15 R. Rumelt, 'Theory, Strategy and Entrepreneurship' in D. Teece (ed.), *The Competitive Challenge: Strategies for Industrial Innovation and Renewal*, Ballinger Publishing Co., Cambridge, 1987.

8 DEFENDING MARKET SHARE AGAINST A NEW ENTRANT

1 G.L. Urban and J.R Hauser, *Design and Marketing of New Products*, 2nd edn, Prentice Hall, Englewood Cliffs NJ, 1993.

2 G. Day, *Market Driven Strategy: Processes for Creating Value*, The Free Press, New York, 1990.

3 H. Gatignon, T.S. Robertson and A.J. Fein, 'Incumbent Defence Strategies against New Product Entry', *International Journal of Research in Marketing*, 14 May 1997, pp. 163–76.

4 J.R. Hauser and S.M. Shugan, 'Defensive Marketing Strategies', *Marketing Science*, 2, 4, 1983, pp. 319–60.

5 G.L. Urban and J.R. Hauser, 1993, op. cit., Chapter 17.

6 J.R. Hauser and K. Wisniewski, 'Application, Predictive Test and Strategy Implications for a Dynamic Model of Consumer Response', *Marketing Science*, 1 (Spring), 1982, pp. 143–79.

7 ibid.

8 ibid.

9 J.H. Roberts, C.J. Nelson and P.D. Morrison, 'Defending Market Share Against An Emerging Innovation', Working Paper 95-006 (April) 1995, Australian Graduate School of Management, University of New South Wales.

10 ibid.

11 J.H. Roberts and G.L. Lilien, 'Explanatory and Predictive Models of Consumer Behavior' in J. Eliashberg and G.L. Lilien (eds), *Handbooks in Operations Research and Management Science: Marketing*, vol. 5, North Holland, Amsterdam, 1993.

12 V. Mahajan, E. Muller and F.M. Bass, 'New Product Diffusion Models in Marketing: A Review and Directions for Research', *Journal of Marketing*, 54, January 1990, pp. 1–26.

13 J.H. Roberts, C.J. Nelson and P.D. Morrison, 1995, op. cit.

9 THE EFFECTIVE LEADERSHIP OF CORPORATE CHANGE

1 D. Turner and M. Crawford, *Change Power: Capabilities That Drive Corporate Renewal*, Business and Professional Publishing, Sydney, 1998.

2 ibid.

10 STEPS TO THE FUTURE

1 See, for example, J.L. McKenney, D. Copeland and R.O. Mason, *Waves of Change: Business Evolution Through Information Technology*, Harvard Business School Press, Boston, 1995.

2 A publication which combines the Fujitsu Centre's work with that of other leading researchers around the world is C. Sauer, P. Yetton and Associates, *Steps to the Future: Fresh Thinking on the Management of IT-Based Organizational Transformation*, Jossey-Bass, San Francisco, 1997.

3 A fuller account of the competencies approach can be found in Sauer, Yetton and Associates, op. cit., Chapter 6.

11 STRATEGIC MANAGEMENT OF VALUE-CREATING NETWORKS

1 Adrian J. Slywotzky, *Value Migration: How to Think Several Moves Ahead of the Competition*, Harvard Business School Press, Boston, 1996.

2 ibid., p. 4.

3 C.K. Prahalad and Gary Hamel, 'The Core Competencies of the Corporation', *Harvard Business Review*, 68, 3, 1990, pp. 79–91.

12 VALUATION AND FINANCIAL STRATEGIES

1 We would like to thank Elizabeth Fulcher for her useful comments on this chapter.

2 I. Fisher, *The Theory of Interest*, Macmillan, New York, 1930.

3 H.M. Markowitz, 'Portfolio Selection', *Journal of Finance*, 7, 1952, pp. 77–91.

4 W. Sharpe, 'Capital Asset Prices: A Theory of Market Equilibrium Under Conditions of Risk', *Journal of Finance*, 19, 1964, pp. 425–42.

5 F. Modigliani and M.H. Miller, 'The Cost of Capital, Corporate Finance and the Theory of Investment', *American Economic Review*, 48, 1958, pp. 261–97.

6 F. Black and M. Scholes, 'The Pricing of Options and Corporate Liabilities', *Journal of Political Economy*, 81, 1973, pp. 637–54.

7 A survey of some of these applications may be found in C. Smith, 'Applications of Option Pricing Analysis' in J. Bicksler (ed.), *Handbook of Financial Economics*, North-Holland Publishing Co., Amsterdam, 1979.

8 This figure is adapted from T.A. Luehrman, 'What's it Worth: A General Guide to Valuation', *Harvard Business Review*, May–June 1997, pp. 132–42.

9 T. Copeland and J. Weiner, 'Proactive Management of Uncertainty', *McKinsey Quarterly*, 4, 1990, pp. 133–52.

10 This figure is adapted from M. Grinblatt and S. Titman, *Financial Markets and Corporate Strategy*, Irwin/McGraw-Hill, Boston, 1998, p. 580.

Index